A Curiosity of Cats

ACKNOWLEDGMENTS

The Preservation Foundation wishes to acknowledges the hard work of the authors in this collection and extends its thanks to them for permission to use their stories.

Special thanks also to Sherry Loller and Kae Bender for copy editing and to Steve Laughbaum for design.

A CURIOSITY OF CATS

Twenty-nine Prize Winning Stories
For Cat Lovers by Cat Lovers

Edited by

Richard Loller

THE PRESERVATION FOUNDATION, INC.
Nashville, Tennessee

A CURIOSITY OF CATS

Copyright ©2001 by the Preservation Foundation, Inc.

PRINTED IN THE UNITED STATES OF AMERICA
First Edition

ISBN: 0-9625798-1-5

Liibrary of Congress Cataloging-in-Publication Data

A curiosity of cats : twenty-nine prize winning stories for cat lovers
by cat lovers / Edited by Richard Loller.-- 1st ed.
    p. cm.
  ISBN 0-9625798-1-5 (pbk.)
  1. Cats--Anecdotes. 2. Cat owners--Anecdotes. I. Loller, Richard.,
1941-
SF445.5 .C87 2001
636.8'0887--dc21

                    2001002986

Additional copies can be purchased at bookstores
or on the Internet at our web site: http://www.storyhouse.org
Richard Loller is at preserve@storyhouse.org
Send conventional letters to:
3102 West End Avenue, Suite 200
Nashville, Tennessee 37203
U.S.A.

Editor's Note

This book is the result of a contest. The contest began January 1, 1997, and continued until we had enough good stories to publish as a book. On December 31, 2000, it ended—152 stories later.

Why cat stories? We began the program with prizes for fiction and nonfiction. But in the first few months we got so many cat stories we broke them out and decided to set up a separate prize.

But just who are we and why are we doing what we do?

The Preservation Foundation is a nonprofit corporation established in 1976. I got the idea when I was general books editor at Abingdon Press, the book publisher for the United Methodist Church.

Like all editors, I had too many manuscripts to read and too little time for reading them. So I learned to cull them quickly. I could decline most after reading the first few pages. Why? Because they weren't for our market. Despite all we could do, we got piles of inappropriate manuscripts. We even got a book of bawdy jokes! I read it all the way through, I must admit, but still it went back.

In fact, it was often true that many of the most interesting projects were the ones that had to be declined. And it wasn't just because we were a religious book publisher.

Many interesting projects were simply too limited in market to interest any publisher who had to justify acceptance on the bottom line. A vast majority of such books were biographical or autobiographical in nature. They were usually by writers who wanted to tell their story or the story of someone they admired. Yet, unless the writer was a storytelling genius, the sales side of the table at publication committee meetings would have an unanswerable objection: "Who's gonna buy it?" In fact, even if a writer is Shakespeare reborn, it seldom happens that she hooks up with just the right editor. Sadly, the typical project makes its slow rounds, rejection slips pile up, and the author grows discouraged.

So, back in 1976 I founded the Preservation Foundation, a nonprofit corporation. My idea was simple. Good writers ought to have a way to preserve and share their works without humbling themselves to a trade publisher or getting cheated by a Vanity Press.

Since 1976 a lot has happened.

Back then, when words were set in lead type, it was a mysterious and expensive process to get a manuscript through all the steps required for it to become a book. Today it is so simple that most books could be produced on this computer I'm using.

Still, the process is time consuming. And I was too busy to devote much time to the idea. I became a stockbroker in 1979 and the demands of that profession didn't leave much time for publishing. Now, however, I've reached a point where I can afford to give more time to the Foundation.

So, in 1997 we established Writer's Showcase, our web site. That's where you can read the one-hundred-twenty-three other cat stories that aren't in this book.

In 1998, our first year on the Internet, we put over one hundred stories up on the site. Today we have stories from Greece, China, Australia, England, France, Hungary, Poland, Canada, India, and from all over the United States. These stories can be enjoyed by readers anywhere. This is the realization of our purpose.

Yet we are still at the beginning. In the future we hope to establish a way to continue the work after I am gone. We want to be sure that these works really will survive for the enjoyment of uncountable generations to come.

Make yourself a part of this idea.

To learn more about us and to find out how you could help, visit our website or contact me by E-mail.

Creative people are capable of turning good ideas into reality. The Preservation Foundation is a good idea. Thanks to members, like the ones in this book, it will someday become a reality more grand than any of us can now imagine.

It is beginning. It is growing. Join us.

Richard Loller   http://storyhouse.org
Nashville, Tennessee   preserve@storyhouse.org
May 7, 2001

To
Dorothy D. Bass
Whose early support and encouragement
made this book possible

CONTENTS

THE BATMAN COMETH

John Bailey

In which Harry Cat breaks the law repeatedly, causing much alarm and disorder. But it all comes out right in the end.

"I say, can you spare a minute to talk?"

The squeaky voice caught me completely unaware, so much so that I nearly dropped my pipe. A towering, scrawny-looking man had come into the garden and round the back of the cottage to confront me in my favorite sitting place. Talk about soft-footed - I'd not heard a sound before he spoke.

"I'm sorry... I know we've met, but..."

"Kevin. Yes, we met a few months ago over at Gelli. Billy calls me the batman. Sorry to intrude, but it is very important."

There's something about life in the deep country that makes people think there's no such thing as an intrusion. No matter what you're doing, it's customary to drop it at a moment's notice and be welcoming and hospitable to any passer-by. It's not a bad custom. In fact, when you've been alone for hours, days or even weeks without speaking face to face with another human it's a very welcome custom. So, although I'd been deep in thought, enjoying the evening, I smiled my very best all-purpose smile.

"No problem at all. Coffee?"

"Oh, thank you, no. I need to show you what the problem is." And off he walked around the front of the cottage, me trailing meekly behind him.

"Look," he said, pointing up at the attached garage roof. "This won't do at all, you know."

I looked to where he was pointing. I couldn't see anything amiss. There was Harry Cat, perched on the ridge, intent on something that, so far as I was concerned, was nobody's business but his own. The roof looked sound. All seemed in order.

"What won't do?" I said, puzzled. "What's the trouble?"

"It's your cat. You'll have to stop him doing it."

"Doing what?" I was getting a bit edgy. It was a lovely, quiet evening and I couldn't for the life of me see what was wrong with my little bit of the world.

"Catching Pipistrels. They're a protected species, you know."

"Pipistrels?" I looked up. Suddenly the penny dropped. "Oh, you mean bats."

And, sure enough, living up to his reputation as a hunter, fabled far and wide, Harry made a scooping gesture and picked a bat seemingly out of thin air. A quick bite and it was limp, and the murderous little puss disappeared over the ridge, carrying his prey with him.

"There, you see?" The batman's voice grew even more squeaky, and he'd gone pale with horror.

"Yes?" I was a little on the defensive now, feeling a bit like Dorothy shielding Toto from the wrath of the wicked witch.

"Your cat is breaking the law!"

Visions of Harry in the dock swam before my eyes. I could hear the magistrate thundering doom... No, this was all too silly for words. It was clear, though, that the batman was truly upset and I didn't feel I could turn the whole thing into a fabulous joke. Though it was tempting.

"Oh, I see what you mean." I didn't, but a little white lie doesn't hurt when politeness controls circumstance. "Let's go and have that coffee and talk about it."

We sat, steaming coffee by our sides, discussing ways of preventing Harry from hunting Pipistrels. Overhead in the gloom, the bats were out in their hundreds, riding the standing wave that lifts over the ridge on which the cottage perches, snatching flying insects from the air much as Harry, in his turn, plucked the bats themselves when they came his way. So far as I was concerned, Nature was working, nicely balanced, and the valley was feeling good.

I waved the batman down the lane as he drove off, mollified and content that I'd do my best to correct the law-breaker.

Looking up, there was Harry, perched on the ridge again, waiting. So I stood and watched. He seemed to be studying the fascia board on the adjoining roof most intently. We both waited. And waited. Just as my mind was wandering, a velvety black blob oozed out from under the board, took wing, and was snatched out of the air by a triumphant cat.

Harry had found the bats' front door!

My laughter raised the echoes. Harry paused, dead bat dangling, and gave me a despairing look, wondering what was wrong with the silly old coot now. And I'm sure that the other furred and feathered inhabitants of the valley paused for a moment to study me covertly as they went about their evening business.

That night, as we sat in front of the fire, I gave Harry a good talking to. He just smiled and looked at me sideways. He was right of course. I decided to let Nature take its course.

Sure enough, a few days later, doing my dusting chores in the attic bedroom, I realised that something was missing. The soft, comforting scratch and snore of the bats in the roof void was absent. The bats had flown. I rattled the rafters. Silence. No, the bats had definitely flown.

They do that. Any observer of Nature will tell you that bats will suddenly vacate a roosting place when it becomes unsafe. And having a baticidal cat lurking outside your front door is a good definition of unsafe, if you're a bat.

That evening, as I sat watching the light fade, Harry joined me, gave a big sigh, and curled up on my lap. We watched in silence as the bats poured out from their new home high in the big oak tree just a little way down the valley. They were out and about, taking station, beginning their nightly feed.

I looked at Harry. He looked at me. Sideways.

"Oh well, Harry, at least the batman will be happy now."

Harry studied a paw closely, gave it a half-hearted lick, and kept his silence.

KILLER CAT

Arnetta Baugh

I was four years old the warm spring day my little sister was born. I spent the day on the farm with my grandmother. That same morning, grandma's big gray tabby gave birth to four kittens, two black and white ones, one gray marbled one, and the last one yellow and white striped.

"Do you think I can have the yellow striped one, Grandma? He's so cute."

"We'll have to ask your mom when she gets home from the hospital, Lindy."

Grandma lived on the farm next to ours, so every day I walked to her house to play with the kittens and watch them grow. When the kittens were weaned, I brought the tiny yellow one home and named him Tom-Cat.

Mother reminded me, "No animals in this house, not even a kitten cute as this. You can keep him on the back porch. I put a box out there for him to sleep in. I have baby Sarah to take care of, Lindy, so you'll have all the responsibility for its care."

"I will, I promise, Mama, I will. I'll take good care of him."

I tiptoed into the house, past the sleeping baby, to find my favorite doll blanket, the one with teddy bears on it, and tucked it in the box. Three or four times a day, I carried out a bowl of warm milk and some table scraps for him.

After I started kindergarten, Tom-Cat became so lonesome he took up with the chickens. He slept with them at night, often scaring away the skunks that came there looking for eggs.

Tom-Cat let me carry him around for hours. His lanky body hung out both below and above my arms. When he decided he'd had enough of my play, he'd lick my hands and face with his sandpaper tongue, making me weak with laughter.

I could never ride my favorite Appaloosa, Blossom, without Tom-Cat pressed between the saddle horn and me.

He never killed any of the robins or sparrows that nested in our apple trees. He was, however, good at catching mice. He would play with them, toss them in the air, let them go and tackle them again and again; finally, by the tail, he would drag them under the porch out of sight.

I gave up playing with dolls, because I had Tom-Cat to dress up in my doll clothes, complete with bonnet, sweater, and socks. I'd put him in my doll buggy and away we'd go.

"Ooh, Tom-Cat," I'd croon to him as he lay back on the pillows and blankets. "You look so cute all dressed up. You really are my baby, aren't you?"

One Saturday afternoon in August when I was seven, two of my friends and I were running through the sprinklers when mean old Mr. Larsen came rushing into our front yard yelling, "I'm gonna kill that damn cat of yours. Been eatin' my chickens. Scatterin' feathers from hell to breakfast."

I ran into the house. "Daddy, Daddy, come quick. Stinky old Mr. Larsen's out here and says he's gonna kill Tom-Cat."

My father jumped up from the table where he was reading the newspaper. "No one's goin' to kill Tom-Cat, Lindy." He pushed up his shirtsleeves past his elbows and charged out the door. "What's this all about, Fred?"

"Your cat killed some of my chickens."

"That's not possible and I'll show you why."

Daddy hugged me, held my hand as we walked toward the chicken coop. Mr. Larsen followed us into the backyard, into the cool of the shaded chicken coop. Just as my father expected, there, sound asleep, was my precious cat all snuggled in a nest with one of our chickens. Daddy reached for Tom-Cat and scratched his ears, waking him. Tom-Cat stretched, jumped out of the nest and came over to me. I picked him up and gathered him in my arms.

Mr. Larsen hung his head, laughed, "I guess you're right, Ray. That can't be the cat I saw. This cat's a chicken lover."

Dad and Mr. Larsen strolled away from the coop. Mr. Larsen slapped my dad on the back, "Where'd you ever find a killer cat like that there?"

"I knew you couldn't hurt any of them chickens, Tom-Cat." I hugged my best buddy. He gazed up at me with his large green eyes, purring contentedly.

A MATTER OF FAITH

Kae Bender

A piece of red yarn held the cat in check as the two little girls clambered out of the Toyota's back seat. They tumbled over each other and their own feet. Peggy called goodbye over her shoulder to her mother. She pulled a knit cap tight over her blonde curls to keep out the biting wind that had sprung up.

Melissa's wavy brown hair whipped about wildly in the wind. She tried to toss a wayward strand back over her shoulder with an impatient flick of her head. The action only further disturbed the gray and black tabby cat in her arms. The cat squirmed and tried to pull out of the girl's possessive grip. Melissa nuzzled her suddenly cold nose into the cat's neck. She crooned to the cat, "Do you want to stay outside, Samantha? It's getting awfully cold!"

"Come on! Put her down and let's go!" Peggy interrupted, tugging impatiently at her companion.

"Wait, Peggy! I've got to untie this yarn first!"

The long red string dangled from the cat's flea collar. Melissa tugged at it, but the knot held firmly. Finally, she bunched the cat in her arms, took the long piece of yarn in both hands, and pulled; the yarn tore apart raggedly, leaving a short stub firmly knotted to the flea collar. Only then did she set the cat on the ground.

Samantha raced frantically across the yard to the woodpile at the back of the lot. Giggling and talking, the girls hurried into the house and stomped up the cellar stairs. In the warm, steamy kitchen above, Melissa's mother heard the commotion.

"Melissa? Is that you? Mark called. They're going over to Jerry's later, so he wants to eat early. Bring up that six pack and put it in the freezer. Mark'll have a fit if it isn't cold!"

Mark and Melissa's mom had only been married a few months,

and Sue was always trying hard. On the cellar stairs Melissa wrinkled her nose and grimaced at Peggy. Maybe she could keep Peggy over for dinner again as a buffer against the discomfort. She whispered in Peggy's cold-reddened ear.

Giggling, the girls burst through the doorway, sighing with relief as they entered the warm room. "It's cold out there!"

"I know; at least the beer won't be hot." Sue bent over the stove to check a steaming pot. Melissa mimed wiping her brow, then scowled as Peggy started to laugh. Without looking up, Sue went on, "It's supposed to get down to the teens by night. Where's Samantha?"

"Outside."

"Well, I guess she knows what she can take. At least she'll be in when she's ready to eat!"

Melissa turned from the refrigerator. "Can Peggy eat over? What's for dinner?"

Sue paused to turn down the stove. She was glad to see that at least one member of the family was making friends in this new environment. She laughed in relief, answering, "Spaghetti, and I don't see why not. You two are certainly inseparable lately!"

As both girls ran down the hallway to call Peggy's mom, Sue grabbed another place setting and rearranged the table. Fixing the salads, her thoughts drifted. She mused about how things had changed since her whirlwind marriage that past summer. Mark had certainly swept her off her feet and into another world. A lump formed at the back of her throat. Sue dismissed the unformed thought by swallowing purposefully and turning her thoughts to the cat. It was hard to believe that Samantha had only joined the family eight weeks before. She seemed as much a part of their routine as Mark -- and easier to accommodate.

It had happened just before Thanksgiving. Someone down the block was moving, and the confusion had disturbed the family's cat. Like any good mother, the cat had taken her babies away from the danger, and the four had ended up in the vacant lot behind Sue's house. The kittens had come nosing around the back porch to check things out.

Melissa had spotted them right away. "Oh! Look! Kittens!"

Sue remembered glancing out the window, wondering where these bits of fur could have come from. They had seemed so tiny; but when Melissa begged to be allowed to feed them, it became obvious that they were no longer nursing.

Cute and playful, the kittens drew lots of attention, but when anyone approached, they ran quickly back to the edge of the woods. The mother cat set the example, and none of her kittens would let anyone touch them. It was the next afternoon before their owners were identified. Linda from next door came over. "Have you seen some kittens out here?"

she asked Sue. "The Coreys' moving men scared off their cat and her kittens."

"Oh, so that's where they're from. We've been giving them a little milk. Melissa was afraid they might be starving."

"I thought I'd seen them back here. Anne asked me to put out some food over at our place, but that stray we feed must of scared them off. Let me give you some food for them."

Sue smiled, "Thanks. I didn't know what cats eat. Mark said they're carnivores, so we gave the mother a little leftover steak; but the kittens seemed too small." She took the plastic baggie of cat food. "When will the Coreys be by to pick them up?"

"Tomorrow, I guess," Linda had shrugged.

"Great," Sue had replied, calling after Linda, "Thanks for the cat food."

And Linda had gone home, leaving Sue to cope with her daughter's growing affection for kittens who would be leaving soon.

But tomorrow came and went with no Coreys. Soon the girls had named all the kittens: There was Patches, the calico; Shadow, the almost white, definitely not gray, but somehow sooty-looking male; and, of course, Samantha, the dark striped tabby. From the beginning, Samantha had been the friendliest and, Mark said, the smartest. Of course, maybe it was really just the most curious. At any rate, when Sue called them for dinner, Mama -- as the girls called the mother cat -- came, bringing her three kittens. But it was only Samantha who ventured near the people when the meal ended. And even she dashed away when they came too close.

A week went by with the girls and the whole family becoming familiar with the ways of cats. It was almost a disappointment when the Coreys finally came; and when no one could capture the elusive cats, the girls celebrated a reprieve.

Another week went by, with the cats living in the woods and eating on the back porch. The girls didn't let their chance slip by. Slowly, very slowly, they crept closer and closer to the kittens until two were caught and kept inside overnight. For the next week the game continued, until Samantha seemed to allow herself to be caught with increasing regularity. She became affectionate and responsive, and by the time the Coreys again returned, she had captured the hearts of the entire family.

Sue chatted about the girls' naming the kittens as they made one last attempt to find the calico. Mrs. Corey must have taken this as a sign of weakness and -- with only the shadowy male already spoken for – sensed a likely sucker. She offered the cat -- for free. Sue would have gracefully declined, but Melissa and Peggy prevailed with imploring eyes. "Ple-e-e-ease! We'll take care of her. We'll feed her and clean up after her and play with her. Can't we keep her?"

Even though she foresaw herself taking care of the animal once its newness wore off, Sue convinced herself it would be all right. After all, Mark didn't seem to mind the tabby.

"Oh, all right. We'll keep Samantha, and since we can't seem to find the calico, I guess we can take her for Peggy-- if your Mom will let you!" Sue had agreed, to the ecstatic delight of her young petitioners.

And so they had become a cat household.

Over the weeks that followed, Sue's internal predictions came to pass: she fed the cat; she cleaned up after the cat; she tended the cat and looked after her. And insidiously, she began to grow fond of the cat.

Likewise, Samantha learned where her bread was buttered. She wound around Sue's feet when Sue walked, she purred when Sue approached, and she jumped onto Sue's lap and gently kneaded her chest with soft paws when things were quiet at the end of the day.

In the weeks that followed, life returned to normal. After the first unnerving days of having a cat, things settled back into routine. Only now the routine was slightly altered. Instead of the alarm waking Mark for his day at work, Samantha meowed loudly from the cellar stairs.

Instead of scraping plates into the disposal after dinner, Samantha's dinner plate was filled. Instead of skipping the pet food aisle at the grocery store, Sue clipped kitty litter coupons and added cat chow to her shopping list.

The girls came in from school and played with the cat. They picked up library books on everything you need to know about cats and training your cat. They put the cat out and let the cat in. And pretty soon it seemed like there had always been a cat.

So after their spaghetti dinner, like any other night, the dinner scraps went into Samantha's dish. But this time, unlike other nights, the dish went untouched. Samantha didn't push open the doggy door and climb the cellar steps. She didn't fling herself at the back screen and scratch up a ruckus that got the door opened. She didn't meow loudly and wake up the family. She didn't come home.

In the morning, Melissa worried about the cat. "It's so cold. Where would she sleep?"

"Don't worry about her, Honey," Sue soothed immediately. "Cats have their own built-in fur coats, and nature takes care of them in the cold. Remember when she was a baby? Her mother taught her how to live in the woods. She'll be back soon for her breakfast." Reassured, Melissa went off to school, and Sue went about her daily chores.

Since she and Mark married, Sue hadn't worked -- not so much by choice as by constraint due to the job market in the small town where they had moved. It irked her to be unable to find a job when a career had been so much a part of her life for so many years, but Mark approved. Wholeheartedly. To please him, Sue had let her applications dwindle, though her ambition continued to tug at the edges of her conscious; and, even though unemployed, Sue would tell her friends when they infrequently called, she was never out of work! So Samantha was not an item of continual concern during that first busy day. In fact, it wasn't until Melissa returned from school that Sue realized that Samantha still hadn't come home. Even as doubt and worry began to invade Sue's mind, she calmed her daughter, promising that Samantha would be back shortly and in fine shape.

"Perhaps someone saw her out last night and worried that she was cold, so they took her in," Sue reasoned. "And they just haven't put her back out again yet," Melissa nodded, satisfied. Her concern evaporated and off she went, content in her trusting faith.

Sue, on the other hand, sat with the mending on her lap and Samantha on her mind. She worried. What if Samantha were injured? What if the meat she had the other night had gone bad before Samantha got around to eating it and she was lying somewhere with food poisoning? What if some sadistic boys had found her? What if she were stuck up a tree and waiting to be talked down, as had happened before? There were so many things that could be wrong. If only she knew. She just hoped that Samantha was okay.

Mark arrived home for dinner just at twilight. Instead of coming in quietly through the cellar, he raced up the back steps, a beer already in his hand, and pulled open the kitchen door.

"Sue! Com'ere quick!"

She ran to the door, drying her hands on a dish towel. Fear clutched her stomach and clouded her face. Her mind raced, frantic that Mark had stopped again for one too many with the guys and now the police were on his trail. She hurried out onto the back patio, glancing furtively up the driveway.

"What is it?" She pushed her hair back from her eyes with the back of one hand to follow his pointing finger. Up in the branches of a very tall oak tree in the woods behind their lot was a huge bird. Annoyance mingled with the relief that flowed through her veins. She had seen the bird once before, from the breakfast table as she sipped her morning tea, sitting in unemployed tedium, trying to stretch the grocery budget to accommodate Mark's taste for jumbo shrimp and fresh-squeezed orange juice. That morning, she had first thought that it was an owl. Then later she thought maybe it was a hawk. Now, it was merely relief. It wasn't the problem she feared and it wasn't a dead cat.

Automatically, she fixed Mark a drink and told him about the missing cat. He shrugged and downed a long swallow. His reaction was

19

not what she expected. A smile dawned in his eyes, "D'you know what hawks and owls eat?"

"Mice?"

"And little cats."

"Oh, Mark. I won't think that." Sue's eyes darted around the kitchen, looking for something to distract her. She busied her hands stirring the macaroni.

Mark changed the subject abruptly, "Where's Melissa?"

Sue shook her head. "She and Peggy are out circling the block looking for the cat...But they should be back any minute!" she added hastily, remembering that when they weren't eating right away, Mark expected Melissa to be there to entertain him. He had developed a habit of teasing Melissa and tickling her and laughing at her discomfort. Hearing their laughter from the kitchen, Sue had thought at first that it was genuine affection; and Melissa, after so many fatherless years, had loved the attention. But lately, Sue noticed a reluctance on her daughter's part and a growing propensity to invite Peggy to stay for dinner. On those days at least the episodes were skipped or the humiliation shared. And Sue now realized, even with the cold, the two girls were spending most of their time outdoors.

When Melissa and Peggy came in just in time for dinner, they had no news to report on the cat. With barely washed hands, they sat down to plates piled high with macaroni and cheese, chatting animatedly about their adventures. They had been all around the block, but no one had seen Samantha. They had even mapped out a plan to continue the search the next day around the surrounding blocks.

"We told them our address but not our names," Melissa assured her mother proudly.

Sue was shocked. Such training they got in school these days! "They're your neighbors! I don't think it would hurt to tell them. After all, they live just houses away!" The girls squirmed uncomfortably. Melissa had been raised in the city. Her mother would certainly have been proud -- then -- that she had remembered her lessons so well. "Well, they know where to come if they find her anyway!"

The dinner conversation palled for a moment, but soon thoughts of discomfort and of Samantha were forgotten. Life went on.

It was pitch black in the bedroom when Sue awoke. She turned and squinted at the illuminated dial of the digital clock.

4:54

Did such a time really exist? She rolled over and tried to return to the deep sleep from which she had been dragged, but thoughts of Samantha assailed her mind. At least she wasn't dwelling on Mark so much.

20

As the days went by, her list of what-ifs had grown. None of them offered much comfort. She lay quietly on her own side of the wide waterbed, alternating worries. She wondered when she had stopped finding comfort in Mark's arms, when she had stopped reaching out across the expanse of tightly stretched sheet to nestle against him -- and why he never did either. She hated this bed with its heated, undulating depths that never left her feeling warm or loved. Sue felt tears forming for all that was missing in her life. She told herself that she was crying because Samantha was still lost.

The sky outside the curtains grayed to a wintry dawn. Mark came awake, chatting beside her. Seven o'clock already? She sluggishly crawled from between the covers. It never ceased to amaze Sue that Mark could wake so buoyantly, seemingly unaffected by the alcohol he consumed every night.

She never functioned well in the early morning, whether she drank or not. Even when she had to get up and off to work, her staff had always left her alone to wake up with her morning tea. She put her hand to her head and winced at the noise.

"You know," Mark said in his pert morning banter, "I never thought I'd miss that silly cat waking me up every morning, but I do. Dumb thing, going out and getting herself killed like that."

"Oh, Mark. Don't say that. You have to have faith! I've been up for hours worrying about her."

Sue took two aspirins.

Sue got the family breakfasted and off to their daily activities. With a load of laundry in the washer, she geared up in hiking boots and parka to brave the wind chill for another walk through the woods in search of the cat.

She wasn't sure what she was looking for or what she hoped -- or feared -- she would find, but she scanned the ground and called plaintively, "Samantha!" There was no sign of the cat. No footprints in the frost. No bits of fur or trail of blood. No body. No response from the quiet forest except the tiny scuffing sound of birds.

Sue commuted between the laundry room and the woods all morning, but again to no avail. She peered into the woodpile. She walked along the property line. She traipsed through the undergrowth, dead in the winter cold. She called and looked and searched until her feet were numb and her teeth chattered endlessly.

From the warmth of the kitchen, she continued her search with her eyes and her mind. But in her heart, Sue knew it was over. She reached for the phone book and dialed the Humane Society, the Rabies Unit, the Sanitation Department. No stray cats had been reported in her neighborhood. No dead ones had been picked up either. No news. Now it was just a matter of time.

She stared outside aimlessly, at a loss what to do next. The house work didn't tempt her away from the ordeal. In desperation, she pulled the want ads section from the heap of morning paper scattered on the table in front of her. It had been weeks -- maybe months -- since she had scanned the columns.

She was tired of waiting. Waiting for Mark's income to improve. Waiting for financial security. Maybe it was time for her to take the initiative. At least checking out the ads felt like progress.

There was nothing ideal, but Sue circled three items anyway and set up her typewriter facing the kitchen window. She typed distractedly, leaping up at intervals to explore still another false lead. She even checked the tube leading from the drainpipe, remembering that Samantha and Patches had once played in it when they were kittens. No stuck cat. No cat. Nothing.

By dinnertime, the letters were mailed, but her last threads of hope for the cat were fraying. Another dinner that Samantha had missed. More than two weeks. Too long.

Mark popped open another beer can; "Face it, she's been here every night for dinner since she was a baby. She just isn't coming back."

Mentally, Sue agreed. She was almost ready to concede defeat. "I suppose you're right." But even as her rational mind was giving up, her inner self clung to the desire to hope. She scraped the dinner dishes into the trash, a sigh of resignation pulling her shoulders down.

Her next morning settled into its boring routine: Sue sat at her desk, trying to pay enough bills without overdrawing her checkbook. It hadn't been hard at first, when Mark was still bringing home the money he had promised. But soon after the wedding, things started to go wrong. First, he said, the interest rates were up; then he talked about the end of the year slump.

Sue wondered if other salesmen had as much bad luck finding qualified buyers. Commission sales just weren't all they were cracked up to be. Sue would have preferred a smaller but steadier income. The wild fluctuations from month to month and the seasonality of it all were a constant struggle. She had always been used to a steady salary and felt naked without a bank balance.

For a time, thoughts about money preoccupied her; but after a while, her mind strayed back to the cat. She found herself wishing there was someone she could confide in, someone to talk it all over with; but since they had moved in, she had barely managed to meet the neighbors, let alone make friends of them. Housewives were an alien breed, and she was lost in a small town. She felt isolated and alone, without even a cat to comfort her. She sighed.

Her memory took her back to another time when all had seemed hopeless. Her mother had been a Girl Scout leader. She had planned a special outing for her troop, an overnight trip to Philadelphia for the Fourth of July. The plans were made, the reservations in, the money raised, the permission slips signed. But suddenly, the money was missing. Two hundred and eighty-six dollars collected from a sale of hand-crafted afghans the girls had made, gone.

They had searched everywhere: the bags, the books, the car, the room where the troop met, the route from there to home -- everywhere. The money was lost. There was no hope of replacing it. The trip would have to be canceled.

But just before they were ready to call the girls, the troop's co-leader, Marjorie Bainbridge, had slapped her forehead, "Of course! Don't call yet! We can try Saint Anthony!" Sue remembered her mother's look of confusion. They weren't a religious family, and saints were the farthest thing from her mind at a time of trouble. Words had tumbled out of Mrs. Bainbridge's mouth about times when Saint Anthony helped people, rescued the situation, found things for people. The stories about people her mother knew were almost persuasive.

When Sue's skeptic mother had still looked unconvinced, Mrs. Bainbridge had gone on, "You just promise him money if he helps you find what you've lost. It won't cost us a thing if the money doesn't turn up." And somehow her mother had agreed to try it. After all, what had they to lose? They promised the saint a reward to help them find the lost money, to let them take the girls on their long-planned trip, to save the day.

And sure enough, half an hour later, there it was. An envelope full of ones and tens and change. Stuck in the side pocket of her mother's purse, right where they had looked at least seven times before.

Saint Anthony. Sue considered the thought. She could give him a try. But that was silly. She didn't even believe in God. How could she believe in something as silly as a patron saint of lost things? Still, what did she have to lose? Sometimes it helped to believe even if it was silly. Maybe he found cats as well as money.

A fickle ray of hope flickered in her heart. But then her blooming hope faded as she recalled the other time she had tried Saint Anthony.

She was newly separated then, with the baby not quite three. Living in a ground floor flat in the city, scrimping and saving, adjusting. They were doing all right, just the two of them. That night, she had come in from work, tired as usual. Melissa had been restless after a hectic day at the preschool, but as Sue prepared dinner in the kitchen, the apartment had grown peaceful and quiet. How it escaped Sue's notice, she was never sure; but when dinner was ready, she called Melissa--and got no response.

Sue went into the bedroom to find her daughter. Instead, she was met with an absolute disaster area: jewelry boxes open on the bureau, their contents scattered about and Melissa, standing in the midst of the mess, fingering the chains and bracelets on her wrist in absorbed abstraction.

"Oh, Melissa!" Sue had shouted in exasperation. Melissa had jumped in startled surprise, not quite falling from her perch on the chair she must have laboriously dragged up to the chest. Discarded jewelry lay about everywhere -- on the dresser top, in the drawers, on the floor. Rings and pins and earrings. Sue took pity on her little daughter and went over to rescue her from the chaotic disarray.

Patiently, she told Melissa, "These are Mommie's. We need to put them away now."

Obediently, Melissa helped. Soon all the rings and things were collected and sorted and stored back where they belonged -- everything but Sue's diamond engagement ring. Sue had searched over the drawers and floor again and again. She moved the chest and turned back the rug. She shook out Melissa's dress and undershirt. She got down on her hands and knees and peered under the baseboard. Finally, she said to Melissa, "Did you see a ring like this?" -- and showed her daughter one with an oval-shaped stone -- "only with a white stone in it?"

Melissa nodded her head gravely.

"Do you know what happened to it?"

Again Melissa nodded.

"Can you tell Mommie?"

Melissa nodded. "I had it and I put it on my finger."

"Where is it now?"

"I dropped it."

Patiently, "Where?"

Melissa, who was still standing on the chair in front of the chest, pointed down.

"Right here?"

Melissa nodded again.

"Did you see where it went then?"

Melissa nodded.

"Well?"

"A monster came and took it."

Wonderful. Sue sank down on her bed and buried her face in her hands. It hadn't been a great marriage, but the ring had been nice.

So she had tried Saint Anthony, offering him money, promising more than she could really spare. Again and again she had tried. But nothing had ever happened. They never found the ring. When they were

24

packing to move one time, she had found a rhinestone in one of the packing cartons, and she had wondered in passing if that was Saint Anthony's idea of a joke. But she couldn't really believe in him.

Now, here she was, half a dozen years later, with nothing to believe in and no hope left for her cat. With her luck, if there was a saint, he would just dangle a substitute in front of her -- like maybe a picture of a scrawny tabby in the Humane Society weekly ad. Still, she had nothing to lose.

After all, she had tried everything she could think of to do on her own. Sue stared into the fire and turned the search over to the saint, mentally promising Saint Anthony money if he would find her cat -- in good health. She paused. But did he do animals? Maybe, she added, he could get -- who was it that did animals? She wracked her brains -- Saint Francis, was it? Anyway, she promised her saints money; she even explained how she'd send the money to church with Peggy's mom, who was Catholic. And she reminded them that she couldn't believe if there was never any reason to hope.

She peered out into the darkened yard. Nothing moved. She woke up early and listened. No cat called from the cellar. She scanned the roadside as she drove along. No animals scurried in the underbrush. She gave up the search. Her saints had failed her.

The next day, she shopped, avoiding the pet food aisle. At home, she put away the cat toys that still littered the family room. She took apart the scratching post and packed the catnip away in a box. She washed the cat's dishes and put them away. She took the order form for the name tag and the application for a Friends of Animals spaying certificate and filed them in her desk. She packed up the bags of cat food for the Humane Society but decided to wait until after dinner to throw out the cat food containers she kept accumulating in the freezer.

The school bus dropped Melissa at the corner. Sue went to meet her at the door, "Keep your coat on. We have to get these books back to the library, and then we can swing by the Humane Society to drop off..."

Sue was distressed by the look of sadness that overwhelmed Melissa's little face and slumped her whole young body into an attitude of defeat. It filled Sue with compassion to see her daughter feeling as hopeless and depressed as she did herself. She wanted desperately to fix it all for her. To undo all the wrongs she had committed in running -- ruining? -- their lives. Sue burned with the sad acknowledgment that there were things she just could not control. Things that she, on her own, could never make right. She thought about the loss of the cat and hated to admit defeat. She realized that she had been refusing to admit defeat about a lot of things lately. Things that maybe she could do something about -- things she could change. In that instant, Sue resolved to do everything in her power to rectify the mess she had made and to make up to Melissa for the pain her mistakes had caused. She hugged her grieving daughter in understanding, a silent promise of love rebinding them into the team that they had always been before. "I can't do it all by myself," Sue heard herself say, "but things will be all right."

Melissa's eyes hid tears, and she nodded in despairing hope.

They dawdled at the library, slowly looking over the stacks. Melissa finally picked out a book about a Valentine cat. At last, they could delay no longer; they drove on slowly, neither commenting on the glorious flaming sunset.

As Sue pulled open the door to the Humane Society shelter, a small sign in the window caught her eye. "Business Manager needed. Information within." Hope again tugged at her heart. Maybe things worked out for the best after all. Even without the cat, all was not lost.

The receptionist greeted them warmly, with a smiling "What can we do for you today?"

Sue felt the hope prickle along her spine. "Well, two things really. First, our cat has disappeared. It's been several weeks, and I just don't think she'll be back." Sue felt Melissa stiffen and slip away toward the kennels. Blindly, Sue thrust the bags of cat food onto the counter, "We thought you might be able to use this."

The receptionist thanked her profusely, and Sue smiled awkwardly, trying surreptitiously to wipe her brimming eyes. "Um, also, I saw the sign in your window?" Sue trailed off at the blank look from the woman behind the counter. Feeling suddenly unsure of herself, she went on, "I've been a manager -- before. When I lived in the city. And I was, well, just wondering about the job?"

"Oh, of course," understanding dawned in the other woman's face, "the help wanted sign. That's not for us. It's from the Society. Not just this shelter. We have five other locations around the county -- plus the administrative office downtown. Let me get you the sheet the headquarters people left about it. You can call them for more..."

A shriek interrupted them. Sue raced toward the kennel, sure that a mad dog was ravaging her baby through some flimsy wire fencing.

"Mommie! Mommie! Quick!"

Melissa's urgent cries echoed through the empty dog room where Sue instinctively sped, searching for her child. All thoughts of jobs and lost cats were abandoned. Fear and panic battered at her heart as Sue skidded into the cat room, letting the voice lead her. She stopped short, collapsing against the heap of her daughter's frail body.

No vicious beast was tearing Melissa limb from limb. No rabid teeth marks punctured her exposed skin. No fear or panic at all -- only her joyous daughter, pressed against the wire cage, nuzzling a gray and black tabby cat: a tabby that stretched its paw through the wires, touching the girl's coat, her arm, her face, anything that came close enough to reach -- a tabby with a bit of red yarn dangling from its flea collar.

Moments behind Sue, the receptionist came, fearful of the scene that had caused such heart-rending cries. Hand to heaving chest, she paused in the doorway, arrested by the tableau of mother and child -- and cat. The little girl sprawled across the floor, fingers entwined in the cage wires, whispering welcoming noises to the obviously responsive tabby cat; the mother knelt, hugging her child, with tears of joy sparkling in her eyes.

"Oh! You found your cat!" the receptionist beamed. It didn't happen often enough. "You're really lucky, you know. We got that cat in not five minutes before you arrived."

All the way home, Melissa crooned to the cat, checking the black tip of her tail and the leopard spotted belly and the little bit of red yarn still knotted to the flea collar. Sue smiled and went straight to the kitchen to fix a bowl of milk and a dish of leftovers. But first, she stopped at her desk and tucked away the shelter's job announcement.

Tomorrow, she thought: There's hope for tomorrow. Then she found an envelope and slipped in all her cash, sealing it tightly. Across the front she wrote with a flourish: "Saint Anthony."

THE CLAIMING OF THE SHREW

Tracey Q. Bush

By the time our kitten, a spirited, cream colored Tom dubbed "Parker," was twelve weeks of age, my husband and I decided that now might be the perfect time to present him with a playmate. However, while it might sound as if this decision were made with Parker's best interests in mind, in reality our motives were purely selfish. You see, although Parker could, at times, be very affectionate, he was also displaying behavior that distressed us. Let me put it this way; at one point my arms were so full of scratch marks that a friend asked if my new pet was a mountain lion!

Later, during one of Parker's checkups, I asked our vet where I might find another cat. Well, it just so happened that someone had recently deposited a litter of orphaned baby kittens at her office door. While

27

two were already spoken for, there was a little multicolored female who was looking for a set of parents. So, with the blessing of my husband, we planned to welcome the new kitty, Gwendolyn, into our home as soon as she was old enough to get a clean bill of health.

One month later, the fateful day came when Gwendolyn was set to join our family. To spare Parker any distress, I scheduled an appointment for him with the vet for that same day, so they might have a chance to become acquainted. Though, before I even saw Gwendolyn, our vet choose to warn me that she had a reputation for being a spitfire and how she might end up being quite a handful. But, when they brought her to me, she looked so tiny and harmless that I thought to myself, "How could such a sweet kitten be any trouble at all?"

Well, I soon discovered the answer to this question - the hard way! You see, I had high hopes that Parker and Gwendolyn would immediately hit it off, and become a feline version of Romeo and Juliet. Instead, they behaved like Petruchio and Katherine from "The Taming of the Shrew!" Thus the story of their stormy courtship is an amusing bit of high drama I like to call, "The Claiming of the Shrew," which goes like this…

Act I

Parker and Gwendolyn's initial meeting at the vet's office went rather well. Though they only saw each other for a few minutes before they were placed in separate carriers. However, on the ride home, Parker seemed annoyed because Gwendolyn was traveling with us. Once home, I sat both their carriers down and opened the doors. The two cats cautiously walked up to one another, until Parker threw the first punch. Gwendolyn, in response, ran for cover - until he cornered her in a hallway.

As he hovered over her, he seemed to be saying, "Hark maiden, bow down before me, for I am the mighty Parker-master of all you survey! And you, my sweet, are destined to become my bride!" Then, assuming that he had frightened her into submission, Parker gave her a quick swat on the head.

To my amazement, Gwendolyn seemed not all that impressed by Parker's efforts to empower her. Instead, she choose to stand her ground and slapped her claw-ridden paw across his face as if to say, "Back unworthy knave! For I am Gwendolyn, and I bow down before no Tom! I am Kitten, hear me roar!" Then, they stared one another down, until I felt forced to move them to separate rooms, with separate accommodations.

Act II

Try as I might to help Parker and Gwendolyn bond, my efforts all seemed to fall short of my expectations. And, while Parker wasn't exactly thrilled at the prospect of sharing his turf, he always treated Gwendolyn in a manner which insinuated that he was smitten with her. She, in turn, spurned his advances and took every opportunity to chase Parker out of his own litter box and food dish, yet still he remained her ever persistent suitor. Thus, even in their most heated exchanges, Parker would appear to be saying, "Try as you might, sweet Gwen, your resistance only renews my vow to win your heart! Mark my 'Meow's.' One day, my fiery shrew, you will be mine!"

To which Gwendolyn seemed to reply, "Eatith Crow!"

Act III

Two days had now passed since Gwendolyn's arrival, and still no progress had been made. Sadly, their mutual inability to get along still forced me to, for the most part, house them in separate rooms. Though, while I had at first taken this course of action for fear that Parker might hurt Gwendolyn, suddenly the shoe was on the other paw. Now, whenever she might catch him napping, Gwendolyn would dive, whiskers first, into his stomach, in hopes of instigating a knock-down, drag-out grudge match. And, with all the finesse of a pro-wrestler, she would dare Parker to "Bringith it on!"

Act IV

At my wits end, I took the advice of a friend who suggested that the more I kept Parker and Gwendolyn separated, the less of a chance I would have of them ever getting along. So, this certain morning, I let them roam the apartment together. I was expecting WW III, but then, something amazing happened. Instead of fighting back, Parker let Gwendolyn do as she pleased. If she started a ruckus, he walked away from it. If she crowded him out of his food dish, he simply went to hers. In short, like Petruchio, Parker had come to the conclusion that the best way to win the love of this most difficult female, was with reverse psychology. So, instead of fighting fire with fire, he greeted her outbursts with kindness, and hence captured her heart. So moved was she by his decision to treat her as an equal opponent, Gwendolyn proclaimed, "Noble suitor, for your efforts to accept me as I am, I allow you to claim me for your bride!"

On a closing note, the trials and tribulations of Parker and Gwendolyn's courtship clearly echo the sentiment of William

29

Shakespeare, who, in A Midsummer Night's Dream, observed that "The course of true love never did run smooth."

Tribute To A Wise And Playful Soul

Kim Celli

A year and five months ago, my cat, Nicki was diagnosed with fibrous sarcoma. Over the last year and a half, we've been through six surgeries, a lot of medication, and even more tears. Sadly, it's finally caught up to us, and the cancer has spread through Nicki's ten-pound, tortoise-shell-colored body. She's developed a new tumor just above her left front leg, which appears to be growing in size each day and has caused her to develop a limp. The pain of watching the cancer spread through her body is excruciating, but not as painful as knowing that there's nothing I can do to help her. Nothing to do but sit back and watch this disease take her away from me.

Nicki has been a constant in my life for eight years. She follows me through every room of the house, waits patiently in front of the tub while I shower, sleeps with me each night, sprawls on my stomach to watch television and is, at this moment, sitting on my lap with her head resting on the edge of the keyboard as I type. Through all of my problems, broken relationships, jobs, and moves, Nicki has been with me. The reassuring rumble of her purring against my ear and the steadiness of her green eyes when she gazes at me has anchored me and brought me back from some pretty terrible places.

This morning I broke down. It wasn't the type of crying that I've experienced in the past, but the kind that leaves your entire body sore and seems like it may never stop. In the middle of the jag, I kneeled in front of Nicki where she was lying in her favorite spot on the bed. Placing my head against the bed, I clasped onto her fur, holding on for my life, and sobbed. Through my tears, I could see that she was staring at me quite thoughtfully, blinking her large, owl-like eyes in confusion. She'd never seen me carry on like this. After some time of watching and sniffing my hand, she apparently came to an assessment and a course of action.

You kinder, gentler animal lovers would probably guess that she curled up next me, rubbing and purring to comfort me. Or perhaps you're anticipating that she licked my tears away. And while that would be a satisfying, endearing conclusion to my story, that's not what happened.

That cat bit me!

I was shocked at first. I stopped crying, looked at her, and said, "Now why did you go and do that?"

But that was just the beginning. She grabbed hold of my hand with her pointy little teeth and started gnawing. Then, putting her furry little feet against my arm, started to kick me; the whole time with her back arched, fur standing on end, and this wild, devil-may-care look in her eye; if you have a cat, you KNOW that look.

Through accusing, tear-stained eyes, I said to her, "What about all the belly rubs and table food I've given you? What about all the thunder storms I've protected you from? Have you forgotten the time when I jumped in front of that truck to save your furry little butt from being run over? Or the time I didn't yell at you for beating the crap out of that snotty Persian cat next door? You forgot about that, didn't you? I'm going through some kind of breakdown and this is what I get? What is this – some act of 'tough love'?"

But my indignant outrage just seemed to spur her on. In time I found myself laughing as I batted back at her paws and curled my hand, mimicking a claw, to dive-bomb her belly with a playful attack. And somewhere in the middle of it all I saw her reaction for what it was. Nicki wanted me to play with her. It was as if she were saying to me: "Yeah, I know both of us haven't been feeling so hot lately, but let's just say to hell with it and play!"

She had a point, so I took her advice. We played despite the fact that rolling around must have made her leg hurt and that she tired easily these days. We played despite the fact that my nose was running and what I knew of the world was crashing around me. We played despite the fact that the time I had left with this precious creature was running out.

Despite all of it, we played.

Alamo Encounter

Mike Crifasi

Cats know nothing of the human condition, nor would they care if they did, I think. They are free animals, quite content to roam wherever and whenever they choose, with not a thought as to anyone else's concerns on the matter. They tread upon whatever gains their fancy - their only aims their own amusement and, occasionally, survival. Perhaps that is why we humans look upon them with such awe and such longing.

As I sit here in San Antonio, it is those thoughts that are passing through my head. I'm in the Alamo, one of the most somber reminders of human cruelty and destruction still standing upon American soil, (bravery as well, but we always remember the worst of it first, don't we?), sitting on a bench across from the memorial wall. This is where I was able to find a much needed rest from trudging along after my companion through the old mission. My companion is quite the history buff and appears so enwrapped in the experience, that he has not even noticed my absence from his flank. I am quite happy to be able to slip away, and I doubt if it would bother him at the moment if he knew.

It's not as if I don't understand or appreciate the depth and impact of this place, nor do I have anything but the deepest respect for those who gave their lives to let this place have a mark in history. It's all just a little too heavy for me, leaving me feeling drab and depressed. I suppose I'm too emotional to look at it all objectively and with interest. It just seems too sad, so it brings me down.

So here I am, on a rather pleasant Sunday morn in San Antonio, looking at the mission walls and rich vegetation within this historic site, resting my weary legs and feeling, well, a little down…

All of a sudden, I see it.

And I can hardly believe my eyes.

Making its way between the small ferns planted before the wall covered in maps and names, disappearing and reappearing behind the legs of tourists who pay it no attention, is a feline with smooth black fur and white patches. My heart lightens as I gaze in amazement at what seems to be such an out of place visitor. It stops and sits up, its tail swaying lazily from side to side behind it, right across from the little bench to which I have laid temporary claim.

I can still not get over my shock that such a creature would be found on this hallowed ground. I am also quite unaware that this new presence has swept away my disillusionment, although I'm sure some small part of my soul is very thankful for that. I sit up a little myself, interested in what the cat will do next.

It just continues to sit and stare at me, tilting its head a little to the side, as if more amused by my attention than I am surprised by its entrance. Its eyes have that squinted look that means in people that the sun is bothering them, in cats that they are either coming from, or on their way to, a delightful nap.

OK, so we have acknowledged each other's presence, but what now? Like too-shy teenagers in the thralls of young love we continue to sit there. I am in my own small way, a "cat person," so I do what any person of that guild would do, I attempt dumbly to call it over to me.

I also continue to stare right at it, hoping that it can somehow sense in my stare that I am a companion, a kindred spirit. While my gaze holds its focus, I lift my right hand just the smallest bit from its perch upon my thigh and begin to rub the first two fingers and thumb together gently, in what I guess must be a universal cat-call motion. I don't really expect much out of it, it generally just leaves you feeling dumb as the cat eventually walks away to look for something more interesting to play with, like a bug, but it gives me something to do, something better than dwelling upon history of my own kind sometimes best left forgotten.

That's when my new feline friend surprises me. After another look, head nod, and further squinting of its sea-green eyes, it begins to walk towards me.

A few nearby tourists take casual notice (not my companion, of course, he's still too deeply entrenched in who shot at whom where and how many times). Right now all my attention and consequential excitement is placed upon this strange cat, that somehow, I am getting to come and spend time with me.

It reaches me and stops. It then looks up at me with a curious stare and sits. I stare back and it seems like an eternity before I notice it doing the signature bunching up move cats do before the are about to spring upon something. After a few good moments of preparation, it leaps onto the bench beside me.

The cat stands there for a moment, apparently still trying to decide if it really wants to trust me, holding its ears back and its body prone. Then cautiously, it leans forward, raises a paw with white ends like a sock, and lays it upon my leg. The rest of its limbs are soon to follow, and all of a sudden I have an unknown cat in a strange city going about the immediate business of rubbing against me and requesting petting attention. And who am I to deny that?

Rubbing behind its ears, under its neck, and along its back, I continue to be amazed at this small miracle. Maybe I just like cats more than the next person, maybe I just crave companionship, but regardless, I tell you, this cat purring under my touch is bringing me more happiness than anything else I have come upon today.

People have turned to look. Passerbys who have happened to witness the encounter comment softly about the cuteness of the situation. It's the same reaction the newborn brought into the relative's room for the first time receives. Now the whole congregation of people about the wall are watching our interaction, even my companion, who is also my father (and finally looking like it as he raises the camera for what I note in my mind as sure to be a refrigerator masterpiece when we get back home). I don't need to look up from my endeavor, and the contented feline pays no heed to anything but finding the best angle from which to receive maximum strokeage, but I think we both feel the power of our simple act of trust has accomplished.

A whole group of strangers: young couples, old gentlemen, and the occasional wide-eyed child, have turned from their attempts to feel the impact of one of their kind's tragic events, to the greatness of an everyday event at hand. They have been taken from their distance and been brought together by seeing two alien parties come together over nothing but pure goodwill and the wish for some simple enjoyment. And in those minutes, not one of them has a care that they remember, and nor do I.

I pet the cat some more, and eventually the bliss passes, (people never let themselves be happy for too long, they have been taught too well to feel guilty when they leave their problems behind). The onlookers move on, my father turns back to his wall and his names. After a final look, he begins to move on too, telling me warmly that it's time we finished our tour.

A sadness washes over me as I finally admit to myself that I will eventually have to leave this new friend. Still it is totally unlike the cloudy haze that had gripped me before the cat strolled so casually into my life. It is a bittersweet twinge in my soul, a knowledge that while leaving it to continue its roaming and care-free life will hurt, I will always carry the memory that we spent this magical time together, and for a while our experience touched lives other than our own.

I stroke its length one more time and then stop. It opens its eyes and looks up to me, and I swear it was saying without having to speak that yes, it understood everything I had thought and felt, and that the impact had been the same for it too. It's as if it understood and accepted it better than I myself in that infinite wisdom any cat person can tell you felines have. The hope from that thankful gaze, I think, I will keep with me always.

I set the cat down and after a final grazing of my legs, it moves on, tail raised and swaying gracefully.

I rise and smile after it, thanking it in my mind and wishing it a good journey, whatever that may be. I move on, feeling all the better that it has touched my life, however briefly, and believe for the moment, at least, that somehow, everything, from now on, will be OK.

I Once Knew The King Of The Forest

Krissi Danielsson

I once knew the King of the Forest.

Picture this: a little four-year-old girl with flowing brown hair, no cares in the world, and believing in everything and nothing. Her whole life lay ahead of her, and her emerald eyes were filled with stars brighter than any shining in the midnight sky. She loved the world, the trees, the grass, the squirrels...and she rarely had an unkind word for any soul save her little brother. Then one day, the girl steps outside into the cool autumn air, and among the flowing dandelions and crunching leaves, she sees before her the most charismatic little tabby kitten...

When I met the King of the Forest, he was very young. He belonged to one of our neighbors, but he spent most of his time with me. He would see me across the street and come running with the instant recognition of a face that loved him. He would follow me around, sometimes waiting until I'd pick him up so he could crawl purring up onto my shoulder.

I was, of course, his only weakness. The rest of the world was his to conquer. All the woods behind the house in which I grew up were filled with creatures that knew his place in the hierarchy. He would walk right up to the meanest dog and give it a whack in the nose, a whack the dog would never forget. He challenged and won battles with skunks and loose neighborhood dogs, regardless of physical size. I still remember the day he chased an arrogant cocker spaniel through the parking lot in a hilarious moment that I still remember to this day.

One day, the little four-year-old girl's neighbors moved away but left their pet. The King of the Forest didn't mind. He could subside on mice and squirrels, and he could spend his days hunting in the woods and conquering new lands in the forest. Yet, he had other things in mind. He loved the little girl. He started spending time on her porch, waiting for her to come out to pet and love him, and he began bringing the little girl's parents offerings of dead mice in an attempt to win their hearts.

The mighty hunter eventually won over my parents. Kings always get what they want. When my family adopted him, I was about seven or eight years old. It was one of the happiest days of my life, on almost equal ground with my wedding day. Growing up in a family of six, suddenly there was someone there who thought I was the most special person in the world. All the pain and hurt of feeling overlooked by my parents, who had to also care for my three brothers, didn't matter so much. There was a friendly pair of green eyes around that stared at me with such love, crawled next to me at night to purr me to sleep, and comforted me when I needed him.

The King stayed at my side as I grew up, almost like a guardian angel. He slept on my belly when I had surgery to fix a broken foot and couldn't walk around. He listened to me throughout the heartbreak of my first adolescent crushes, and he was there to feel my joy the first time I really fell in love. And it was all his choice.

The week before I graduated from high school, ready to head off to foreign lands and see the world, my King of the Forest crawled behind a chair in the living room and fell into a coma. Looking back, I should have suspected something. He had spent every night of the previous week with me. We'd known he was sick. But I'll never forget that day when my parents picked me up early from school so I could have my last chance to say good-bye.

I once knew the King of the Forest. Right now, he's roaming through the sky and chasing away the squirrels in the woodlands of the clouds.

And when I get to heaven, he'll be waiting for me there.

CHARLIE

Gwen DeLamar

I didn't want to write Charlie's story because I knew I would cry. He's been gone for a long time, but he's still close to my heart. After reading some very good stories about other cats, I decided that Charlie needed to be remembered too.

How do I begin to tell about Charlie? He was all cat, Charlie, from the tip of his little pug nose to the end of his ever-swinging tail. Beautiful, is how I'd describe him. Though just a stray, he had the carriage of royalty. His long gray silvery coat sported a white star just under his neck. I could almost imagine that one of his forefathers belonged to a Persian princess.

Charlie loved us as much as a real cat can love humans, but mostly he tolerated us. My daughter and I wanted to hold him and snuggle.

Charlie would tolerate it just so long, then he was gone. On the other hand my husband, Charles, clearly had no interest in Charlie and often made the comment that cats weren't good for anything. I often thought that his resentment towards Charlie had something to do with the fact that Charlie was named after him without his consent.

I once heard that cats will chose only one person in a family with which to bond, and to everyone's dismay, Charlie chose Charles. Each night Charlie would finish his meal, then preen himself for nearly an hour before he jumped into my husband's lap for a long nap. Neither touched the other, they simply tolerated one another.

If my daughter or I tried to pick Charlie up and hold him, he would quickly scamper away and head straight back to where he was least wanted. Charlie was an acrobat too. Many times my husband was almost brought to the point of heart failure when Charlie would silently creep up behind the recliner and jump over my husband's head and into his lap. As many times as Charlie did this, my husband was never prepared for the overhead assault.

There was one game that Charlie would play with my daughter and me, but it took a lot of coaxing. We would stand in front of Charlie and wave our nightgowns back and forth. Charlie's tail would begin to sway. Then he would position himself for the launch by rocking back and forth. Eventually it ended with us screaming and running through the house and Charlie in hot pursuit.

Charlie had a particular dislike for all females, I think. I had a lady that came once a week to clean for me and Charlie clearly hated her. One morning she arrived before I had finished dressing for work, and she had gone upstairs to get the bed linens. Charlie was waiting for her just inside one of the bedroom doorways. The attack was swift and the result was a blood curdling scream that would wake the dead. From that day on, I had to make sure that Charlie was out of the house before the cleaning lady would come inside. Even so, Charlie was not through with her. He knew that she would come outside to put the trash in the garbage can. Charlie was patient. He waited, and he nailed her again. Now she refused to take the trash out.

Charlie lived his life pretty much like he wanted to. If he felt romantic, he would scour the neighborhood in search of female companionship. My sister had a female cat and wanted Charlie to mate with her cat. When the time was right, I grabbed Charlie, put him in the car and off we went to my sister's. Once there, we closed the garage door and stood back to watch the romantic scene unfold. Never have I heard such growling and howling! Back and forth they went under the cars, darting here and there. It sounded as if they were killing one another. This is not working, I thought.

Indignant that Charlie would spurn her cat, my sister said, "Your cat is obviously gay."

"No, not at all," I replied, "Charlie is just a little choosy. We just need to put a small paper sack over your cat's head, that's all."

Charlie and I went home, both a little huffy. So much for that. Never again would I set Charlie up for such ridicule. Then, weeks later, my sister called. Her cat had one lone kitten, and he looked exactly like Charlie!

As Charlie got older he slowed down considerably. He was more content to swish his tail when he saw a bird perched nearby than to go for the hunt. He didn't play the game with my daughter and me any- more. I could look into his eyes and tell something was not right.

After a thorough examination from the vet, I was informed that Charlie had kidney failure. His advice was to put Charlie out of his mis- ery. "There is no cure," he said.

Breaking the news to my daughter was not easy. She was a teenager and to put Charlie to sleep was unthinkable. Every day she would take Charlie to the vet and he would be hydrated. This went on for almost a month, but Charlie didn't get better. I made a bed for Charlie in the utility room. His litter box sat unused. Charlie was too weak to get out of his bed. The only time he was out of it was when he went to the vet.

My husband and I knew that we should put Charlie out of his misery, but my daughter cried and put up such a fuss that we always backed off. Never again will I let an animal suffer that long. Charlie need- ed to go. We needed to let go.

Even my husband who professed not to like Charlie was deter- mined to properly bury him. He had begun to build a coffin for Charlie. Then out of the blue Charlie came out of the utility room. It was the first time he had walked in over two weeks. He slowly came up to me and I picked him up and held him in my lap. For the first time he let me stroke his head without trying to get away. We sat like this for what seemed like a very long time, then Charlie decided it was time to leave. Slowly he walked to the back door and as I let him out, he paused on the deck as he watched my husband building the coffin. He descended the steps, then turned and looked back at me one more time, then he was gone.

Charlie knew that his hour had come, he said his good-byes, then did what all of God's creatures do. He went to his resting place. His little coffin was turned into a planter and over the years has been the home for many bright geraniums, but its true purpose is to remind us of Charlie.

A ROYAL COINCIDENCE

Jennifer Doloski

"Hi," AJ peeked around the corner and rapped on the door. It was early, but Kenneth was usually awake when she arrived.

"You are here today!" Kenneth beamed as he turned away from the window.

AJ noticed Kenneth's suitcase on the bed.

"I'm going home!" Kenneth grinned and, though pleased for him, AJ had to force herself to return the smile. Working in the emergency room, AJ rarely forged meaningful relationships with her patients. Kenneth, however, had come in alone and AJ had remained with him long after the end of her shift. A fall from a ladder had left him with two broken vertebra, and he was lucky to have escaped paralysis. He said that his sister, who lived too far to visit him in the hospital, would come to help him when he was discharged. Some friends had visited often at first, but as Kenneth's time in the hospital dragged on, their visits became less frequent.

AJ had performed her nursing school clinicals in Chicago, and the violence and tragedy that overflowed into those emergency rooms fueled her desire to live in a quieter, less populated area. She applied only at rural hospitals and had started working here, nestled among dairy farms and cornfields, six months ago. Familiar with being alone in a small town, AJ visited Kenneth almost daily, bringing books, magazines and conversation that he insisted did him better than the food they were serving.

AJ had been trying to keep a professional demeanor. She was only just becoming accustomed to the speed at which news traveled and did not want a reputation for hitting on patients. In church, people whom AJ had never met would approach her to ask about so-and-so's injuries or whether or not someone had delivered her baby. Surely by now everyone knew that the nurse who lived in the old Johnson house was a regular visitor to Kenneth Mercer, a farmer and the town's most eligible bachelor.

The two spoke about nothing in particular.

"My shift starts at seven, I ought to get downstairs." AJ stood, for the first time uncomfortable in Kenneth's presence. She had never minded saying good-bye to a patient before now.

"You're sure I can't call you?" Kenneth understood AJ's reluctance but had asked several times whether he could take her to dinner. He was growing fond of AJ in a way he had never before felt. Their conversations had allowed him to truly get to know her without the formality and awkwardness of dating in a small town.

"I just don't think you should, if I had met you anywhere but in this hospital. . ." AJ began the argument that Kenneth had heard several times, and he silenced her.

"Enough said," he rose and shuffled toward her. They stood, inches apart, AJ looking at the floor and Kenneth studying the freckles that danced across her face. He ran his fingers through her curls; she reached up to stop him, but instead held his hand where it rested.

"I'll miss you," Kenneth whispered and AJ looked up, the pain in her eyes betraying her.

The rattling of the dietitian's breakfast cart down the hall reminded both that they could easily be observed. AJ pulled away and shook her head, but Kenneth knew that once she walked out of his room he'd lose her.

He stepped closer again and, placing his hand behind her neck, guided AJ's face close to his. The kiss was strong, furious with emotion, making up for in intensity what it lacked in length.

The cart rattled louder and AJ backed away, wide-eyed, her freckles camouflaged by the blood that had risen in her cheeks.

"Good-bye," she whispered, almost choked. Turning, she walked out the door and was gone.

It had been busy in the ER that day, and AJ volunteered to work a double shift. She arrived home near midnight. Inside the dark house, she was greeted by her cat and the blinking light of the answering machine.

"Hey, Princess," AJ scooped up the purring mass of fur that draped over her ankles. AJ had found Princess weeks before at the side of the road, her fur matted and muddy, one of her paws badly mangled. She had looked so sad and sorry that AJ thought a royal name like Princess would boost her ego. No one had reported losing the animal, so AJ brought a clean, bandaged Princess home from the veterinarian's office. Playful, she seemed grateful for having been rescued.

AJ checked her messages.

"Ms. Reilly, this is the Valley Animal Hospital calling. A young woman called today looking for a cat that matched Princess's description. I told her that you had found a stray recently and would call her."

AJ played the message again and wrote down the number that the receptionist had left. She sighed, grateful that it was much too late to call.

"Oh, Princess, first Kenneth and now you, too?" She thought of

Kenneth's kiss and once again her freckles disappeared under hot cheeks.

The next afternoon, AJ pulled into the driveway of a small, white farmhouse. As she walked the path to the door, Princess in hand and a lump in her throat, a young woman came out. AJ thought she looked oddly familiar, but couldn't place her.

"You must be Abigail Reilly, and this most certainly is Maxine," the woman reached out to pet the cat. "My brother has been away and the neighbors were taking care of things. One day they came to feed Max and she took off into the fields."

AJ nodded, but said nothing. She stood on the path stroking Princess.

"Please, do come in.   My brother will want to thank you."

AJ stepped into the kitchen and as she did Princess bounded down from her arms. The cat knew the place well, and she disappeared to some other part of the house.

"Max!" A man's voice cried. AJ smiled at his excitement.

"Come on," the woman ushered AJ into the living room and there sat Princess on the lap of the most handsome man AJ had ever seen.

"Kenny, I want you to meet Abigail Reilly. Abigail, this is my brother, Kenneth, please excuse him for not standing, he's recovering from a back injury." The phone rang just then and the woman excused herself.

"Abigail?" Kenneth looked at AJ quizzically.

"Abigail Jane, but my friends call me AJ." AJ was smiling widely.

"Well, AJ," Kenneth said, extending a hand which AJ quickly took, "it is good to meet you."

FELINE CARDIAC PAUSE

Sarah Duroy

Cardioinhibitory is a term listed in the medical dictionary, which is defined as "to restrain or inhibit the heart movement." I suffered from this--standing in the back yard, tears rolling down my face, shining a flashlight into the pitch darkness, hoping to see two tiny spheres of reflective glow shining back at me. You see, I fell in love for the first time with a cat. Now I am not saying that this is the first time I ever fell in love. Love has been good to me and that is what got me into this whole problem.

We moved from a suburban neighborhood where all the homes

were so close together that when your neighbor had a barbecue you could open your window and eat meat right off their pit. We opted for open spaces and have a little land of our own. We moved into our new home in the spring and the next Christmas we had my entire family over for an old-fashion holiday at our new house. That first afternoon together we loaded the kids up and drove to a Christmas tree farm about twenty miles away. My mother was with us so that meant we all had to sing Christmas carols as we rode in the back of a trailer filled with hay. As the cold wind butted across my nose I thought of how corny this was. Although I could appreciate the corniness, that scene would linger in my mind for many years after the holiday and kids were gone. This was the last day for the tree farm to be open this season and the pickings were spare. The kids helped cut the tree and we headed back.

Under a small three-sided building with a fire inside was a cage that bore a sign that read "Free Kitten Neutered." I went over, not because of my love for kittens, but just for my love for a baby anything (except a snake). There was a larger-than-a-kitten black cat curled in the corner of the cage. I turned to one of the people wandering around in the area and said, "Where is the kitten?" I was informed that the kitten was right there. He was already a preadolescent cat. I petted him through the wire. My husband, Tommy, asked me if I wanted it and I said no. Now it is at this point when our communication became somewhat impaired. I really did mean I did not want the cat. I never had a cat and considered myself a "not-a-cat person." Our family loaded the tree and left in the several vehicles that it had required to haul us all to the Christmas tree farm.

Everyone went to our home except for Tommy who drove our car to pick up my grandmother. She lived about thirty minutes away and could only sustain a partial day with us. She was scheduled to join in the festivities after we got the tree and before the cookie baking started.

I became worried after Tommy hadn't returned for a couple of hours. When he finally arrived, I opened the door to find him holding the pre-pubescent cat in his arms. He and my grandmother had stopped at the discount store and purchased a litter box, cat food, and a pink plastic mouse filled with catnip. I was surprised, but not shocked. This was a typical move for the love of my life. A very loving, thoughtful man with a huge heart made of gold.

Well, Tad changed our lives. At first he hid under our bed for a few days. We would get a good glimpse of him as he ran to the kitchen to grab a bite to eat and then to the litter box. After a few days he was hanging out with us. He sat on the end table next to me while I read or worked on some sewing. He was small enough to sit among the cluttered necessities of the table, nestled against my cozy chair. That is how he fit into our lives. He lay there with his long black hair shining with the little white spot right on his chin and all four of his paws dipped in white. Tad was handsome and very kissable. I could not walk by him without stealing a kiss on his nose. Tommy would watch this activity in fascination. He seemed proud of the Christmas gift chosen so well. I loved Tad.

Tad and I spent every day together. When my twelve-year-old son went back to school after the Christmas break, Tad and I got to know each other even better. I talked a lot to him and he to me. He was very verbal, or as a non-cat person would say, vocal. He was a strictly inside cat per Tommy's request. This was an attempt to thwart fleas. Tad and I watched the wildlife through the windows. I kept a side window open for him all the time. Every morning he would come sit on my pillow and purr to wake me up for breakfast. We started off feeding him regular dry cat food. There is an entire aisle at the local grocery store devoted to cat food, supplies, and cat toys. It wasn't long before I felt Tad needed a little special dinner treat now and then.

As many cat owners know, you cannot do this. And so there we were living with a cat that would only eat the small gourmet cans of cat food. At six each morning we had a little breakfast together and then I would go out and feed the birds and squirrels some seed and nuts. I would laugh at Tad as he watched out the window. He would salivate and chomp his little white chin up and down as if he were chewing on the tail of a red bird. His excitement peaked with the sight of a large black crow that dined at our feeder every afternoon.

Tad slept in a round bed made of fake lamb's wool. He curled around in it and was just adorable, Tommy and I would stand over him with pride as if he were one of our babies sleeping so sweetly and innocently in his crib. We loved Tad.

I had all those wonderful feelings that true pet owners have. Coming home to find your four-legged friend waiting patiently for you. Having him snuggle up next to you in a chair hoping you wouldn't have to leave again. All the laughter. The uniqueness that made his life different from all other black and white cats in the world. Tad thought ice came from under the refrigerator when someone opened the top freezer door and rattled the ice. He would come sliding on the kitchen floor with his face positioned low and close to the bottom of the refrigerator waiting for the ice to come flying out. I never could get a glass of ice without dropping at least one piece on the floor. He loved to paw swipe that ice around until it disappeared. He was somewhat curious about the smell of toothpaste and would wake from a dead sleep if he heard the bathroom faucet come on.

My favorite characteristic of his was the way he anticipated the opening of a plastic cola bottle. He would jump to the table and wait patiently until the cap was set beside the bottle and then he would paw swipe it to the floor. He carried it in his mouth over to the hard floor where he could paw it around and make noise. Later when we moved some furniture for spring-cleaning we found about fifty caps. I even found Tad up one night trying to get the cap off an unopened two-liter bottle of cola stored on the bottom shelf in the food pantry. He brought us laughter in places I never expected to find.

He was a well-behaved cat. He never tried to eat out of our plates. One day while I was out he did eat half a bag of barbecue pork skins. They didn't sit well on his stomach and he ruined a kitchen mat. He did chew up a pair of Tommy's work boot shoestrings, twice. That was all the real mischief he did.

As spring approached the flowers came peeking up through the cold ground. With the dirt on my hands and the sun on my bare feet in the new green grass, I could see Tad sitting at the sliding glass door watching me. He appeared to be content. It was I who wanted him to experience the feeling of the grass on his paws and the warm breeze rustling his hair, with his little nose stuck in the air sniffing the spring-time.

I regret this move greatly for it caused great pain in my heart and soul. It made me realize how delicate God's creatures are and how we are here on earth for a journey of unknowable length. I picked up my baby, who was about seven months old and still not full size. But he was now big enough to knock everything off the table beside the chair. He had grown and didn't realize how big he was. I placed him on the ground outside for the first time. He immediately nudged a cricket in the wet new grass. As he pawed and played, Tommy and I sat in wonder as we enjoyed Tad exploring the outside world around him. Abruptly, as if star-tled, Tad ran into the wooded area next to our property. We both ran after him, which made him run farther into the woods. We decided to stop chasing him, thinking that if we just let him calm down he would come out on his own. We waited on the porch for hours. Tad never returned.

Water slid down my face as I stood with that flashlight looking for my newest life companion. I worried about all those things that could happen to a naive kitten at night in the anarchy of the woods. The sleep that did come that night was next to the open sliding glass door. Morning came early with no sign of Tad. I had to work a twelve-hour shift that day. I couldn't keep focused on my work. I just wanted to get home and look for Tad. When I did arrive home it was dark. I took the flashlight out onto the front porch. As I stood on the edge of the porch waiting for those reflective eyes while calling loudly for "Kitty! Kitty!" I heard a soft meow. As I turned around, there was Tad sitting on the other end of the porch! Afraid I would scare him away I walked slowly to the front door, opened it, and ran inside and opened the back door. I crawled out on my hands and knees to the side of the house where he now sat. I moved in slowly, as Tommy was retrieving Tad's food dish and favorite small can of gourmet food. Tad walked around us but would not approach. It appeared that in the setting of the outdoor darkness he could not recognize us. He headed back into the wooded area. Both Tommy and I, braving snakes and whatever else lurks in the woods, ran blindly after him. We looked for hours. Tad made no noise at all and did not return home.

I was physically ill. Affected with a weight as heavy as an anchor on my soul, I told almost everyone I came in contact with how my cat had disappeared. I heard every explanation of cat behavior my friends and acquaintances could offer to help ease the pain. I called home several times a day during the next two days while working my twelve-hour shifts. The report was always the same, no Tad. When I got home each night we drove the car around the neighborhood, shining the flashlight, looking for the glowing eyes, calling his name. We had lost all embarrassment. We were just two people yelling for "Tad" or "Kitty! Kitty" at eleven at night.

With the grieving sadness and need to get up and do something to find and bring our Tad back home, Tommy was the first to break. Since he was a police officer and a tough kind of guy he would never let his real attachment to our furry friend be known. But, with such a big heart, this could not remain a secret for very long. He purchased a harm-proof trap. His plan was to place this trap in the wooded area where Tad was last seen and to place Tad's favorite food, whitefish and salmon gourmet, in the back of the trap. Tad should have been hungry and unable to pass it up. This is what we did. The first night Tommy checked the trap around one in the morning. In the trap sat a reluctant-to-leave opossum. Still no Tad.

The next night he set the trap again, closer to the house, in hopes that we would not catch another wild animal. The next morning I was sickened as I peered out the window and saw a dead raccoon lying on his back with all four feet stuck straight up. I woke Tommy to report the horrible news that we had been involved in the demise of a wild animal. Mumbling words of regret, Tommy dressed chaotically and ran to the garage to find a tool to make extricating the stiffened body of this raccoon easier. I watched from the window. As he hesitantly opened the door he must have been anticipating just what happened. The raccoon looked around and ran in one direction as Tommy ran in the other. The trap got stored away that day for good.

Now it was on to the next plan. It was I who literally constructed this plan. I drew a cartoon version of Tad and wrote all the pertinent information along with the fact that there was a monetary reward for his return. I strategically placed the signs at all exits of the neighborhood so everyone coming or leaving the subdivision would have to read them. At least I felt I was doing all I could to find him. My son and I even took a tour of the county animal shelter in hopes that some kind person had found him and turned him in. As we peered with hopeful eyes into cage after cage lining the walls of the animal shelter, we yearned to see that little black face with the milk white chin looking back at us. He was not there.

Day nine and still no sign of Tad. Tommy arrived home from work. I met him in the driveway. He asked me to jump in the patrol car and drive around the block with him. He shined the bright spotlight that was attached to the side of the car as I assisted in looking for Tad's eyes. As we approached a house on the corner, I saw Tad lounging in the front yard on the roots of a huge tree. I grabbed the flashlight as Tommy stopped the car. I approached him very cautiously, keeping the light on him at all times. My heart was full with joy, my soul was full of fear that he would run. There was also a motherly anger around my mental edges. I vaguely remember Tommy standing in full uniform at the edge of the neighbor's but yet stranger's driveway saying something about he didn't think the cat was Tad. I was not going to let him get away this time. As the cat started to run toward the rear of the house, I leaped out and caught him. He struggled for freedom as I scolded him for being gone so long and making us worry. I headed for the car with determination, in a tornado of emotions, when suddenly I realized that the owner of the home had come outside to see a woman and a police officer stealing his cat.

After two weeks I picked up his toys and his food bowl, placed them in his bed, and put all of it away in the garage. It was at this time that the finality and grieving had just begun. He was not coming back. All the kind and rose-colored things people had said to help ease the pain had not come true. He was not out sowing his wild oats, living off the land, just being a cat for a while. We were all very sad. I had dreams of him getting run over by a car. Dreams of finding him on the porch. Tommy was too upset to even talk about him. He felt that somehow we had let Tad down, that we should have protected him more. He was just an adolescent kitten. I carried the same guilt, but tried to smooth it over with words of Tad's determination to be an outside cat, of his love for the wild.

We never really stopped looking for him. I took the signs down at the ends of the street after a month. I prayed that if he couldn't be with us, please let some little girl find him and be pushing him around in a baby carriage and making him drink milk from a doll bottle. That she would pick him up and kiss him on the nose the way I used to do. That when her mother got ice from the freezer for lemonade that Tad would be there waiting for the ice to fly out from beneath the refrigerator.

The long months of summer had begun. I spent the early afternoon lounging in the backyard with a cool drink and a good book for company, my skin soaking in the hot rays, my mind entranced in the plot of the crime novel. I felt a light feathery brush against my leg. Thinking it was the wind, I continued to read. I felt it again and looked down to see a healthy, well-fed Tad pawing at my cola bottle cap. Bombarded with the emotions of this miracle, I escorted Tad into the house for some salmon and whitefish gourmet.

He never told me where he had been and I never asked. I was just glad he had come back home.

LUCKY

Linda L. Faulkner

Jennie Hamilton frowned at the unsightly mess beyond the rail of her back deck. A quick survey of the area revealed just how much work lay ahead of her. Tufts of wild grasses and clover were springing up, infiltrating the azaleas and creeping phlox along the garden pathways.

Any other year she might have been out enjoying this mild April weather, cultivating the moist spring soil and envisioning a season of flowers to come. But this year she couldn't muster enough ambition to tackle the job.

The usual quail chattering and bird songs were absent this morning, leaving the hillside oddly quiet. Only a faint mewing sound broke the stillness, coming from the live oaks a few feet away. She glanced up and spotted a kitten perched on one of the main branches, not much older than seven or eight weeks.

"Just what we need around here," Jennie grumbled, "another animal making a nuisance of itself."

Realizing it had an audience, the kitten immediately turned up the volume. She paused to listen a moment as old memories began to stir in the distant regions of her mind. Memories of another kitten. A lot like this one, come to think of it. Black with a white collar and white paws. And the little girl who found that stray kitten and wanted it with all her heart.

Jennie's parents, however, were practical folks, hardened by the Great Depression of the thirties. They believed that animals were meant for working on the farm and providing food for the table. To waste good

47

money on a pet was unthinkable.

So, with kitten in hand, she canvassed the neighborhood in search of a good home. But after knocking on countless doors, it was becoming obvious that nobody had room in their lives for her precious cargo. By late afternoon only one person remained on her list. A dismal prospect, at best. Mrs. Johnson, the elderly woman who lived alone in the brick house on the corner, yelled at anyone setting foot on her lawn. Jennie wasn't even sure if that old grouch liked people, let alone animals. It was worth a try.

The minute Mrs. Johnson answered the door, Jennie launched into her sales pitch, now polished with pactice.

Mrs. Johnson shook her head slowly. "Got enough animals messing in this yard already. Don't need one of my own. Try the Marshalls across the street."

Jennie's lip quivered as huge tears began cascading down her cheeks. "I did! I tried everyone!" she sobbed. "Daddy says he's going to take Kitty to the Pound. You were my only hope."

The old woman took a long, hard look at the furry ball of golden-eyed innocence staring back at her. Heaving a sigh of resignation, she asked, "May I hold Kitty?"

After a quick examination, Mrs. Johnson smiled knowingly, "I think we'd better call him, Mr. Kitty. But I'll only accept him on one condition. You'll have to come over and play with him, whenever you've got time."

It was the perfect arrangement for all concerned. And although Mr. Kitty lived elsewhere, he was devoted to Jennie. Every afternoon he would wait for the school bus to arrive and drop her off at the corner. Like clockwork. For almost eleven years. Until the day he died.

Jennie's eyes misted, her thoughts returning to the present. "Now I'm the old woman who lives alone," she told the stranded kitten. "But don't you worry, little one. I'll find your owner and have them come get you."

About the time Jennie completed her quarter mile walk to the main road, she saw Greg Parker backing out of his driveway. The Parkers had moved from Los Angeles two years ago to open up a branch of his booming real estate business and to build their dream castle in the foothills.

The neighborhood hadn't been the same since their arrival. Greg earned a handsome profit by subdividing his thirty-acre parcel, leaving nearby residents up in arms over the loss of their rural environment. His children seemed to take malicious pleasure in racing their dirt bikes past Jennie's house, stirring up clouds of dust and leaving ruts in the gravel road. Greg, who loved to mingle with the upper crust, charmed the local elite with lavish parties that lasted well into the night.

Not that she begrudged the man his money. It was his attitude that irked her to the core. When he insisted on planting tomatoes in early May last year, she'd tried her best to warn him. "I wouldn't put those in the ground yet, if I were you. Winter isn't over 'til it snows on the dogwoods."

As always, her neighbor refused to listen. "Now, Jennie, don't tell me you actually believe that nonsense!"

Just thinking about the smirk on his face made her blood boil. Then, about a week later, a whole foot of snow fell on the dogwoods. And Greg Parker's tomato plants!

Greg rolled down his car window and showered her with phony pleasantries, then moved in for the kill. "Say, there's a nice two-bedroom apartment opening up in town. You ought to take a look at it."

She nipped his dream of a sales commission in the bud by changing the subject. "Did anyone in the neighborhood get a new kitten? Got one stuck up a tree at my place."

"Not that I recall, but I'll check around for you."

Jennie smiled at this stroke of good fortune. Giving Greg Parker any excuse at all to contact people was almost as good as broadcasting it live from the local radio station!

"Want me to get it down for you?" he offered. "I can bring my ladder over this noon."

"Good idea, Greg. Maybe it'll find its own way home."

Anna Reinhardt was in the habit of calling Jennie every day around eleven. The two women had very little in common until Jennie became a widow last summer. Anna, having lost her second husband to cancer over five years ago, was now in hot pursuit of a third Mr. Right. She wasted no time in getting to the point. "You know...the singles group is having a dance next Saturday. With a Forties-style band. Why not go with me?"

Jennie groaned at the thought. "I know somebody who went to one of those things. She told me the men our age just about trampled her to death, trying to get to the younger women!"

The hurt silence on the other end of the line quickly became unbearable. "Oh, I'll think about it," she relented.

Minutes later Greg Parker pulled his shiny new truck into the driveway and unloaded an extension ladder.

"Be careful, now," Jennie cautioned as she led him around to the back deck. "Kittens have sharp claws."

He secured the ladder in place with an omniscient smile and began his ascent. "No problem," he assured. "I have a way with animals."

Catching sight of its would-be rescuer, the kitten started backing up slowly. "Oh, no you don't!" Greg managed to grab it from behind, but the startled animal dug its claws into the bark. The instant he freed one paw, the kitten let out a fierce yowl, taking dead-aim at his face. "Ow!" The rest of Greg's monologue was completely unintelligible as he abandoned his mission of mercy and scurried down the ladder.

"I'll get something for the bleeding," Jennie volunteered.

Ignoring her offers of assistance, he fled to the safety of his truck, shouting all the way, "That damn thing is vicious!"

Smart cat, she decided on the spot. I wouldn't trust him either! The kitten was glaring down at her in indignation for sending that barbarian to the rescue. "I should have known better," she admitted with a sigh.

Jennie knew that cats could be downright picky when it came to humankind. Her education in the aspects of feline behavior began shortly after she and her husband moved to the country.

Jennie had married Wade Hamilton right out of college. They took their ambitions to the city, where she hoped to become a famous author and Wade would undoubtedly set Wall Street on fire. It wasn't long before her father-in-law became seriously ill, pleading with his only son to move back home and help run the family hardware business. Jennie eventually took a job teaching English at the high school, and somewhere along the way, the young couple set aside their dreams to get on with the business of living.

Staying in the area was a decision she never regretted. It was a wonderful place to raise a family, with lots of room for children and animals. They had many pets over the years, but the cats always held a special place in Jennie's heart.

Not long after they moved to the foothills, during a rare Sunday afternoon excursion, they found an elegant white cat sitting at the doorstep of some little antique shop. When the owner told them it was a stray, Jennie's husband suggested they take it home with them. On that day she fell in love with Wade all over again.

Samantha proved to be a faithful companion and, thankfully, good-natured with children, since she had to put up with the antics of two mischievous little girls growing up in the country.

After Samantha was killed on the main road, Jennie's young teenage daughters pleaded for a new kitten. They decided to buy one at a pet store this time. As the family circulated the room admiring each charming ball of fluff, one feisty little Siamese male refused to take no for an answer. The minute they walked away from his cage, he began protesting their rude dismissal in no uncertain terms.

"I don't know if you realize or not," the clerk intervened with a laugh, "but that kitten is choosing you."

Jennie knew better than to question feline judgment, and her family agreed. Caruso, named for his amazing vocal repertoire, ruled the house and its occupants for many years.

Wade was about to retire by the time they lost Caruso. Both agreed that the last thing on earth they needed was another cat, since they were going to travel and do all the things they'd been putting off for years. She started collecting brochures and weaving fantasies around the exciting places they would visit. Sadly, only one week after his retirement party, her husband died of a massive heart attack, leaving Jennie alone and bitterly disillusioned with life.

The soft little cries emanating from the branches overhead began again in earnest. Why don't people take care of their animals? she wondered, annoyed that this burden had somehow fallen on her shoulders. The longer that kitten stayed out in the open, the less chance it had of surviving. There were all kinds of predators looking for such easy prey. Hawks soaring overhead. Bobcats. Coyotes. Even raccoons were known to rip a small animal to shreds.

After giving the matter some thought, a method of luring the kitten down from the tree came to mind. She decided to pick up a couple of cans of tuna at the market. Food just might do the trick!

There were three major supermarkets in nearby Placerville, but Jennie preferred to take her business to Gold Country Market, the small family-owned store just down the road. The clerks all knew her by name, and the darkened hardwood interior rekindled fond memories of childhood. In the market, it was like stepping back in time and going home again.

Greg Parker arrived shortly after Jennie, and they bumped into one another at the end of an aisle. She tried not to smile at his bandaged face.

"I found out that cat is a stray. And it probably has some awful disease, so I'm going to have to get a tetanus shot."

"That's too bad. Are you sure it's a stray?"

"Someone dumped a litter of kittens near the Tyler place a couple days ago. They say the rest got run over. Too bad it wasn't a clean sweep. Anyway, I'll call Animal Control for you when I get back to the office."

"Oh, don't trouble yourself, Greg," she told him sweetly, biting back a more colorful reply. "I'll take care of it. I'm still quite capable of wielding a telephone."

"Well, you'd better do it right away, before somebody else gets hurt!" he said, shaking a finger at her as he marched toward the front of the store.

"Just because I haven't got a man telling me what to do," Jennie muttered to the wheat bread, "he thinks I'm helpless!"

She caught up with him again at the checkout stand. While he was unloading his haul of potato chips and candy bars, the clerk made the mistake of commenting on his injuries. Greg immediately took center stage, expounding at length about being attacked by a vicious wildcat on Jennie's property.

As soon as her neighbor was well out of earshot, she couldn't resist amending the story just a bit. "Greg sure hates to admit that a one-pound furball got the best of him."

The clerk picked up a can of tuna and winked. "Is it really vicious, Mrs. Hamilton?"

"Nope!" she barked. "Just a good judge of character!"

Jennie arrived home in high spirits. Figuring that no cat could resist tuna, she placed a generous helping at the base of the tree.

A few minutes later she looked out the back window and saw the kitten pacing back and forth on its perch, crying in anguish. She ran outside just in time to catch a glimpse of the Cahill's twenty-pound tabby waddling away from the empty dish.

"Now what?" she sighed, pondering the ladder still sitting in place by the tree. Unable to come up with any other solution, Jennie threw caution to the wind, inching up the ladder until she came face to face with the notorious "wildcat." This time, instead of backing away, the kitten ran forward and hopped aboard her shoulder for the ride down. Once they were safely on the ground, her small passenger let out a fortissimo purr, a masterful appeal for clemency that made the whole idea of calling Animal Control out of the question.

"Think I'm going to call you...Lucky," she decided, taking the kitten inside for his first meal, "because you're just plain lucky to be alive! We'll have the vet check you over tomorrow and pick up some kitten food. But in the meantime, young man, we have work to do."

Jennie brought her gardening tools out of the storage shed and started weeding the flower beds, while Lucky darted from place to place, exploring his new home with insatiable curiosity. He reminded her so much of Mr. Kitty. Once again she thought of the woman whose unexpected kindness allowed Mr. Kitty to be part of her life so long ago.

Mrs. Johnson later told Jennie that their first meeting had been a real wake-up call, forcing her take a hard look at herself and the sour old woman she'd become. Now it was Jennie's turn to look in the mirror. Life had indeed come full circle.

"Think I'll call Anna this evening," she told Lucky. "No harm in watching the young folks dance, and listening to music that doesn't grate on your soul...is there?"

With that, the kitten scampered up the oak tree, then came right back down again, as if to say, "See what I can do!"

"Why, you little stinker!" she cried in amazement.

No doubt about it. The joke was on her. Jennie threw her head back and laughed out loud, marveling at the uncanny wisdom of this tiny creature. Long before human logic could begin to sort things out, he had managed to find his way to a heart that needed healing.

She scooped up the kitten and gazed at him in wonder. "On second thought, maybe we're both lucky."

BUDDY

Rhonda C. Graves

I miss Buddy. I can't believe I just said that, but I do miss him. Never in my life would I have believed that I could actually become attached to a cat. Cats had always rated low on my list of living things, hovering in rank slightly above rodents.

I'm not sure how it happened. It started out with that same love-hate relationship. The cat loved me for some absurd reason, and I hated it. It was ugly, scrawny, needy, and pesky from the very beginning.

There is no logical reason why it wanted my affection. I yelled at it, chased it, and even though it was obviously famished, I did not feed it. There was a small part of my humanitarian side that felt sorry for it. I don't like seeing anything hungry. However, I knew if I fed it, that would be an invitation for it to stay.

For days, that cat would appear in the window of every room I entered. It didn't follow my husband's voice, it didn't follow my children's voices, the dang cat just followed mine. When I went outside, it rubbed its scrawny body against my leg and purred as if it were getting pleasure from the human contact even though I was giving nothing in return. I just didn't get it.

Leaving school with a terrible headache one day, I drove home and collapsed into bed. My younger daughter arrived shortly and apparently didn't shut the door very well. I was lying there with a pounding headache, not wanting to hear a sound. What did I hear? "Meow." Not only did I hear that sound that I hated, but it was in my bedroom. I jumped up from the bed, snatched the cat up roughly, stomped towards the door, and readied myself to launch the pesky feline half way across the yard. That's when it happened.

53

After the initial shock of being yanked up by the scruff of its neck, that stupid cat began nuzzling my neck and purring, oblivious to its immediate fate. The cat was still not welcome in the house, but by the time I reached the back door, I just set the cat gently on the ground and said, "You can't come in."

When my husband came home from work, I gave him a choice. I said, "Bryan, you have to take that cat to the pound or let me feed it."

He replied simply, "If it's a boy, it can stay."

So there I was, the ultimate cat hater, running outside to flip that scrawny cat over and actually hoping to find certain parts of the anatomy that would allow him to stay. Then I ran through the house yelling, "It's a boy" as if someone special had just given birth. The children started chanting that the cat could stay, and I ran next door to borrow some cat food.

After borrowing some nourishment for the newest member of our family, I sat on the driveway letting the sated cat stick his claws into my sweats, making a comfy place to rest after indulging in cat chow. His purring was ceaseless, and that's when I decided I had a new best buddy. That is how he acquired his name.

I decided that after a week of petting and adequate food, he really wasn't an ugly cat. He was really turning out to be a very pretty cat. His coat became shiny, and he started filling out. He followed me and the children around outside more like a dog than a cat. He chased missed softballs, much like a dog would. Slowly my mind became more accepting of cats in general, and I actually began to love my little Buddy.

As I was getting ready for work one morning, my husband entered the bedroom with a worried look on his face. He said, "I hate to tell you this, dear, but when I came in after class last night to change before going to work, evidently the cat got up on the engine of my truck to keep warm. I didn't realize it until it was too late."

I couldn't believe it. I had tried to get rid of that cat, I didn't want it to begin with, and when I finally succumbed and accepted it and began to care for it, it was taken away from me. I ran, disbelieving, to the door. There was a pool of blood on the driveway, just where my husband had parked the night before. He told me he was sorry, and I knew he didn't do it on purpose--he liked Buddy, too.

He told me he had driven the same course to work numerous times during the night to see if he could find where the cat fell out of the truck. There was no trail of blood leading us to believe he fell out immediately and crawled to the side. He never found Buddy. All I had to remember my cat by was a blood stain on the drive and a chunk of fur stuck to the fan blade of Bryan's truck.

I drove to work numb. I didn't tell the girls--they would have been angry with their daddy. All day long I had a sinking, crushing sensation in my chest. When I got home, all I could see was the stain, even though Bryan had attempted to get rid of it. I couldn't bring myself to empty Buddy's food dish. Besides, we hadn't decided what to tell the girls yet. Days went by, and I couldn't help but feel guilty for the way I had treated Buddy just a few short days ago. I tried to convince myself that it was no big deal. I would remind myself that I didn't like cats, that my mother was allergic to them, that they chased birds from my feeder, and that Buddy hadn't been around long enough for me to have become quite so attached. All of my attempts to console myself were fruitless. I really missed and grieved for Buddy.

A full week after the fateful day, I began to feel better and was able to accept my loss. Buddy would remain a fond memory, and I was thankful for the short time I had with him. By this time, the girls had decided that either a dog or a car had gotten Buddy, and I decided to let them to believe that.

I drove home feeling a little more light-hearted than usual. Pulling into the carport, I hesitated momentarily before killing the engine listening to an uplifting song on the radio. I turned the key off, put the van into park, opened the door, and heard a noise that haunts me to this day.

It was part meow and part cry. I knew it couldn't be Buddy, but I was still compelled to find the source of the pitiful voice. No sooner did I get one foot out of the van until I felt a familiar brush against my leg. I looked down in horror to see Buddy. He was thin again, there were two chunks out of his side, one out of his neck, one side of his face was practically furless, and one eyeball was completely filled with blood.

I knew he needed me more than ever, but I couldn't decide if I should just start running or stand there and throw up. It was then that I gave my husband his second choice concerning that cat. I walked into the house in a nauseated daze, turned to Bryan and said, "You have two choices. You can go out there and shoot that cat or feed it." Unfortunately or fortunately, I haven't decided yet, the children overheard my ultimatum and ran for the door.

Brittany, my older daughter, took one look at Buddy and so eloquently said, "Nasty" and backed into the house.

My younger daughter, Erin, dropped to her knees, gathered that scrawny, bloody cat into her arms and said, "Poor Buddy. You can't help it. I still love you."

It was then that I gained more respect for my child who marches to the beat of a different drum. She had the strength to do something I couldn't even bring myself to do. As she gingerly stroked and nurtured that pitiful cat, I went to the food bowl and poured some food into it, not knowing if he would be able to chew or not.

That night I even made Buddy his very own bed complete with a blanket. I just needed to try to make him a little more comfortable somehow. I don't know how far that injured cat rode in that truck before falling out and slowly making his way home. I wish he could talk and tell me about how he used several of his nine lives.

It took several weeks before Buddy was a pretty cat again. He stayed close to home for awhile. As his confidence and security grew, he followed his instinct and became a wandering cat. His adventures have become longer and longer, and each time I wonder if he's gone for good this time. I miss him when he's gone, but I have learned to accept his nature and hope that he'll grace us with his presence occasionally. When I started writing Buddy's biography yesterday, it had been over a month since I had seen him last.

But you know what? When I got home last night, that dang old cat had come back. It looks like he might have a broken leg, and he's pretty thin again. He ate a lot last night, with one leg tucked normally underneath while one leg stuck awkwardly out to the side. I wonder what he did this time. I wonder if he'll be home when I get there today.

THE GUARD CAT

Robert P. Herbst

My wife Lyudmila and I run a small office supply store here in beautiful Mount Perry, Florida. We try our best to keep things interesting by having various unrelated items standing about in the store. Lyudmila does some sewing and knitting so a portion of our front window is occupied with her works of art. We also have live plants in abundance and a huge old tree which was fished out of a nearby river.

The tree is about twelve inches in diameter and about six feet tall. It has been somewhat petrified, or "lightered", by being in the river for many years. The lightering process tends to turn the tree sap or pitch into a highly combustible material. Scraps of lightered wood can be used to start a fire with a single match, thus it is called "lightered". This lightered wood is also highly prized by the munitions industry who grind it up and use it as a component in their explosives.

We nailed a board to the bottom of this lightered tree and stood it upright in the front of our shop. It isn't very pretty but it is definitely interesting. As a joke we hung a sign on it stating the sale price was three hundred dollars. Believe it or not, there has been some interest in it. I guess anything goes here in beautiful downtown Mount Perry, Florida.

Last but not least, we have a shop cat. The cat is nothing really special, it's a classic example of , "Allycatus Nonspecificus". Among its unusual features is the lack of a tail, and because it's been to the vet for "the operation," it is now a sixteen-pound "Nedercat" (it's neder boy nor girl). The colors are not unusual, being black and white spotted.

Its main occupation, in our shop, is to sleep in the front window where, as it rolls about, it knocks over our displays. In doing so the cat has become an item in Mount Perry, Florida. People come by our shop just to look at the cat and play with it through the window.

All of the above is usual to the point of being mundane. Life goes on here in Mount Perry, Florida, as it would in any other town. Of course the combination of cat, tree and Russian wife are a bit out of the ordinary but not all that much. Writing humor -- now that is weird.

On arriving here from Feodosia, Crimea, Ukraine, the first thing Lyudmila did was to take the cat outside, place it on the ground in a sandy spot next to the building and teach it to go to the bathroom outside. I had trained the cat for years to the litter box and now in only one day Lyudmila had taught the cat to go outside to the bathroom.

She speaks to the cat in Russian and much to my surprise the cat listens to her. It seems to understand what she is telling it. She has even been able to teach the cat to sleep on various pieces of furniture in our house and not on others. This has been accomplished with a great deal of care and patience.

Recently we have had a rash of shoplifting here in Mount Perry. In our shop, as in others, small items began to disappear from our front counter and the window display. It was only natural because even we need an occasional break just like anyone else. This leaves the front of our store vacant briefly while we take care of "business" in the back room.

In order to achieve a measure of protection we have taken to patting the cat on its head and saying the words, "Cat! Guard the front!" We have named the cat "Cat" for obvious reasons.

In the beginning I thought it was kind of cute to do this. Lyudmila, on the other hand, took the situation quite seriously and spent a great deal of time explaining to the cat, in Russian, exactly what was expected of it.

Frankly, I paid little attention except to note she was spending an awful lot of time talking to the cat. It went on for weeks and all the time the cat sat on its favorite chair and stared straight into Lyudmila's eyes the whole time she spoke to it.

As things do happen, there came a day when I had a call of nature and had to once again leave the front of the store unguarded. As I had learned to do, I leaned over the cat, scratched its head and said, "Cat! Guard the front," and headed for the back room.

I had only been gone a moment or so when I heard the most awful yowl from the front followed by the sound of things being turned over in great number. I thought to myself, "The darn cat is in the window display again," and made mental note I would have a monumental cleanup job facing me on my return. With this in mind I was in no rush to get back.

The noise didn't stop, however. It kept going and it was getting louder by the moment. The crashing sounds were now punctuated by screams of pain. Something out of the ordinary was definitely going on in the front of our store. I cut my visit short and raced to the front of the store.

As I burst from the back room through the swinging door I was greeted with a sight which would warm the heart of any retail merchant. There, perched on the very top of our petrified tree was a medium sized man with an expression of sheer terror on his face. In his hand were several items he had apparently plucked from our window display.

At the bottom of the tree was our cat. It was snarling and growling in a most unfriendly and menacing way. Occasionally it would let out a howl the likes of which I had only heard on TV or at the lions' cage in the zoo.

Each time the cat did this, the man on top of the tree would try his best to climb higher. I now noticed the seat of his trousers had been torn and saw other tears in his clothing.

My jaw dropped at the sight of all this and the man on the tree begged for mercy. He cried out, "Please don't let it get me! All I did was to take a few small items! Don't let it get me!"

Casually and with great deliberation I walked forward in the shop to where the telephone was. The cat on seeing me jumped up on the counter and walked over to me. As I scratched its head it sat down and purred for me. "Good kitty!" I said to it and it purred even harder.

"That's a good cat!" I said again.

The man on the tree uttered a curse and began to climb down out of the tree. The cat let out the most terrible of noises and dived for the base of the tree. It must have been my imagination, but I was almost sure the man got another six inches out of the top of the tree. I slowly put both elbows on the counter and leaned forward toward the man on the tree. In my most agreeable voice I said, "Good morning, Sir. How can we help you?"

There were no more curses, just pleading to be let out of the shop without having to go past the cat. I called the police for assistance but I also told them to take their time, my perpetrator wasn't going anywhere in a hurry.

I reached out and reclaimed the items he had taken from our window. It seemed the man on the tree was almost glad to give them back.

Moments later, a policeman showed up. The man on the tree began a long dissertation about how the cat had attacked him for no reason.

The policeman and I looked at each other in utter disbelief. Then the officer said, "That cat attacked you?"

The cat, of course, had long since returned to the counter where it lay by my hand and purred pleasantly.

He went on, "The cat I play with through the window every night? Yeah, Right!"

With a nod of his head he continued, "I know for sure that this cat wouldn't hurt a flea!"

Then the officer turned back to the cat and me, "Well, if you don't need me, I'll be on my way."

The reaction of the man in the tree was instantaneous and predictable, he spilled the whole story about how the cat never moved until he began swiping stuff from the window. Again he begged to be removed from the shop without having to go near the cat.

The officer placed the man in handcuffs and headed for the door. Now I scratched the cat behind its ears again and said softly, "Good Kitty. Nice Kitty." I could feel a wicked, sadistic grin spread over my face from ear to ear.

Puss In Goots

Sue Lange

After the old lady died, things were tough. I hate to say it, but up until then, I had it pretty easy. The old lady and I had an understanding. We hardly ever talked. We didn't need to on account of our understanding with the food and all. I got two squares and all the hard stuff I ever wanted.

Once in a while she'd toss a treat my way. It was great. And for her part, she got all the lap time she ever wanted, whenever she wanted. I was always right there because I liked lap time too. In fact, I don't know if I liked lap time better or meal time. I mean, I'm a lover, not a fighter.

So when the old lady booked and I wound up on the street, things got real slim. So did I. That was one tough year. I started on life number three at the beginning of that year and by the time it was over, I was on number nine.

It wasn't the street life that was so bad actually, except for the cars maybe. Man, I hated cars. That's probably because of the way Sis died. Sis had a way of climbing up the tire of a parked car and curling up in the engine on cold days. She showed me the trick one time, which I thought was the tops until the day I saw her go up in a puff of fur. I've never felt the same about cars since that day. They're good for getting out of the rain or hiding from dogs, sure, but other than that I don't have much use for them. I've lost two or three lives on account of them. Or trucks. Can't say I'm too crazy about motor vehicles in general.

Living out in the street wasn't such a big problem, but the street itself kept me from leaving the neighborhood. You see, I'd have to cross the street in order to get myself out, so I ended up staying in spite of all the other toms in the area. I never had nothing against them cats, but boy, they sure hated me and each other too! They'd sneer at me because I was fixed, but I didn't mind. Sure, I was just as thin as them and my coat had lost its gloss by the second week out, but Jesus, I didn't look nearly as bad as them toms. If they hadn't lost an eye, you can sure bet they'd lost an ear. And alla 'em had broken tails. One poor soul, I forget his name, couldn't even lift his, it was broke right at his butt! I myself had lost most of mine when I was a kit, I don't remember when or how, but my little stub was always up and always proud. Them toms had ridiculous mangy ropes attached to their behinds. And for what reason? Because they were all fighters. Not me.

You could find food anywhere on the street, but it never stuck around for long. The people that lived here were mostly no count and left their garbage everywhere, but between all the toms and stray dogs and such, the good stuff got ate up real fast. So the toms were always scraping. I wouldn't. I'd take up a post somewheres and move in as soon as a dump was made. I got chased off a lot of times, but since I was usually getting in first I managed to get enough to keep myself alive. Them toughs probably ate better, but you couldn't tell on account of all the energy they had to spend fighting for them big juicy scraps. They wound up skinny as me.

And when that plump little orange and white Pumpkin heated up, those cats would cross a driveway to get to a fight. I never participated. Pumpkin was nice and all but she was just a cat. She never seemed too interested in them toms anyways, looking out from her perch on the windowsill, licking her paws. She appeared to be pleasant and what not, but she never gave a thought to all the chaos happening for her benefit in the yard below. I couldn't really blame her for not being interested; them toms were a mess. Every last one of em.

So anyways when I hit year number nine, feeling hungry all the time and mostly very lonely, I thought I'd make a change. I knew I only had one good life left and I got to thinking about the old lady. The street teed me off and so I decided that I'd pull myself together and just cross that street and look for a new old lady. Actually, I wasn't that particular. I like people; anybody would do, not just an old lady. I missed lap time a bunch and that's what I was looking for.

In that neighborhood, I'd seen a couple of tough old toms that seemed to come and go whenever they wanted to. They'd cross the street back and forth at their own whim. They didn't do much fighting and maybe it was my imagination, but it seemed to me that they were fatter than me and the rest of the scraggly bunch. They kept to themselves mostly so I never talked to them, but I sure did watch. You know I watched them, because they had a secret: the secret of when it was safe to cross the street. After watching them for a good-enough while, it appeared to me that they sort of listened up and down the street and felt at the ground and when they thought it tested out all right, they crossed. I tried it myself and found it was true. You could actually predict pretty truthfully when the cars were coming. So I closed my eyes and listened real close and finally ran across that street, and if you can believe it, I made it!

I spent the whole afternoon patrolling the backyards of my new neighborhood. I peeked in windows, listened at doors, and sniffed everywhere. But I couldn't find no old ladies. I came to the sinking conclusion that I'd have to find another neighborhood.

But by now I was getting pretty cocky. Having lost my street fear I decided I'd try another neighborhood or even a few. I got a couple more in and then I had to go and start to panic. I was hungry almost all the time that year but now I was really hungry and I had wound up somewhere without a lot of garbage everywhere. I took this to be a bad sign, especially when I couldn't even smell anything ripe. It was just so clean. I was thinking of turning around and tracing myself back to my old neighborhood, when a black and white crossed right in front of me and said, "What's up, man? New around here?"

Needless to say, I was quite surprised. It was a tom and not only did he not spit at me, he actually was friendly! Turns out, my buddy Socks was fixed too and pretty well happy with himself. He showed me a spot where if I waited long enough, something would turn up. I was amazed. He said the people around here were pretty cool. I mean the trash was scarce and all but the folks took care of the strays in this area.

Socks actually had a home but he liked to be out in the street where the action was. He wanted to know what was going on at all times with the humans, the cats, and even the dogs and squirrels. Socks was real friendly-like. Most of the people in this neighborhood even thought that Socks was their cat. I believe that Socks himself was never quite sure where he lived.

Socks introduced me to another neighborhood tom, Scarecrow, Crow for short. Crow was crazy. He hated people and just about everything else except Socks. He was skinnier than me and in fact, skinnier than any cat I'd ever seen. One guy up the block kept Crow alive, barely, by putting out scraps a couple of times a week for him.

I hung with Crow and Socks for a few weeks. The food was regular, but pretty scarce. I continued to be hungry most of the the time, but I liked running with them guys. We never fought, just roamed around and told stories. They showed me all the great hiding places in the neighborhood and where all the 'coons and skunks hung out. And of course whose dogs were stupid and whose were on the right track was all real valuable information to me at that time.

Meanwhile, I gotta say, I still missed my lap time. Socks and Crow were great buddies, but they don't take the place of a human touch. A human feels kinda like my mother did when I was a kit. That's what made me like the old lady so much. So I was still pretty lonely.

I resigned myself to living out life number nine in this state until one fateful evening just at dusk. The ever-present hunger had provoked me into sniffing up something, anything, when just as I was turning the corner of a garage, I saw him. My guy. He saw me too, just as I turned that corner. I looked him right in the eye and felt something that I hadn't for a long time. I don't know how to describe it, but for a moment because of whatever it was, I forgot how hungry I was. We stared, waiting for one of us to make a move, threatening or otherwise. Finally, my guy said, "Hey kitty."

I'm not real talkative and in fact I learned to be quite wary of humans due to the loss of life number six at the hands of a cruel human and his fireplace poker in his basement. I like humans for the most part, but the #6 life experience showed me that you really can't predict how each one's gonna fry out in the pan once the gas gets turned on. I guess people are just like toms. Anyway, I stayed put and he eventually left around his corner. I hung for a bit and was just getting up to leave when out of the house here he comes with a bowl of something to put a warm smile on my face. I smelled it immediately. It was the dry the old lady used to leave out for me to have my pleasure with. He set it down nice-like and went back inside.

I couldn't help myself, I had it gone in a minute. Again I hung for a while but when nothing else happened I moved on, looking for Socks to tell the story to. Socks was unimpressed, "I told you people are cool around here. I've seen those people. They're nice. They got their own cat so they don't need us too much, but they've always been straight anyway."

Still, I was surprised and in the morning just before I was going to my favorite napping bush, I decided to stop by my guy's house. I don't know why, I just thought I'd try it. I went up to the door he had gone in the night before. And guess what! There it was. That shiny bowl of dry, just waiting for me, pretty as you please. I looked around for my guy and was sort of sorry that he was no where in sight, but I didn't let that stop me. By this time I was starving again and wasn't gonna stand on no ceremony. I didn't miss a drop and turned the bowl over just in case there was something underneath it.

Well, you can pretty well guess I was passing by my guy's house every morning and every evening and I was never let down. He even put a little bowl of water out. It was so small, I just laughed at it. I mean everybody has old pickle buckets out in their backyards just full of water. It's a never-ending supply for Socks and the rest of us. Still I appreciated the gesture even if I didn't need his little bowl.

Sometimes in the evenings, I'd catch him out just before or after he put the food down. Eventually he started to hang out while I ate. Since he hung, I thought I'd hang. He'd sit on the steps of the front porch; I'd lay on the bottom step. It wasn't lap time exactly but it was at least as nice as going around with Socks and them.

About the time I was just getting to really like the guy he made a mistake. It wasn't his fault really; he didn't know. He reached out to touch me right in the middle of my back. Yikes! Like I said, I like people and all, but because of that life number six thing, I can't trust people right off the bat, and a back is pretty risky. It was a sad turn of things because here I was desiring a little lap and this guy is ripe for it, but I just couldn't deal yet, so I whipped around and let him have a scratch. Not hard, of course; my claws were only half out. I didn't need to hurt him, just had to let him know how things stood.

I got ready to high-tail it, I mean I braced for that kick in the ribs that always comes, but it never came. All he said was, "OK, OK baby. That's cool, I get it." I was pretty surprised. Humans are nice and all but a tom is a tom regardless of species and human males are just as mean as a cat. In fact I sort of chuckled at the whole thing because he called me "baby" and must have thought I was a girl. Oh well. We hung a bit more and then he went in his house. I kind of felt sad. I couldn't remember the last time I was in a house. I guessed it was the old lady's so many lifetimes ago.

After that we spent a few weeks doing the evening routine. It was enjoyable. I even met his girl. She lived in the house with him and she was just as nice. I guess it was her cat that lived with the two of them. She was a real cat person. You can always tell a cat person. They go for the spot right away. By the time I had met her, I had gotten over my fear of my guy touching me, so when she went for the spot (directly on the top of the head between the ears), I loved her right away. I'd say we hit it off real well.

Both of them were great. We all got along, but their cat was something else. Now, I got nothing against people or cats. Like I said, I'm a lover, not a fighter, but I've noticed that most cats ain't like me and Socks and the Scarecrow. My guy's cat, Giggy they called her, was more typical of our kind. She'd sit up in the window looking at me, and never a friendly word, not a "hi," nothing. If she made any sound at all, it was just to spit. But she was curious, and jealous! Boy when those two were hanging around with me she would get to cryin' in the window. I just laughed to myself. It was even more funny because she was a black and white, like Socks. And she looked to be the spittin' image of him, but they were nothing alike. Giggy and I eventually came to an understanding but not until a whole lot of other stuff happened first.

Like the incident when the girl went to rub my belly and I had to scratch her. Just like before, it was a knee-jerk reaction because of number six life. After I did it, she felt so guilty that I was as sorry as I could be because I done it and decided right then and there that I'd let either one of them touch me wherever and whenever they wanted. I didn't need to wait no longer to figure it out. I could tell these people were the real thing.

But there was still Giggy, Miss Giggy I called her. She might have been jealous of me, but she had no idea of how jealous I was of her living in that cozy little house. But eventually we did come to our understanding, Giggy and I, but at that time I just regarded her as the loud, mean, and pretty scary cat in charge.

And when I say scary, I mean scary. Giggy was the queen of her backyard. Everyone was afraid of her. My guy and his girl used to put her on a leash so she couldn't run out of the yard. The leash was real long and hooked up to the wash line so's she'd be able to run the whole length, making it out to any corner she wanted. Whenever another cat got close to Giggy's yard, she had a way of making herself look about twice as big as she really was and that face! What a face! Classic Halloween! Giggy was the type of cat you knew had to be a witch in her previous life. Later when I found out she didn't have any claws I had a great laugh about the whole thing. Nobody'd ever seen a cat as old as Giggy, who happened to be thirteen years. Apparently a cat will learn a lot in thirteen years, and how to protect themselves without fighting was one of their big lessons. I liked Giggy and she eventually liked me, but at the time we mostly just tolerated each other.

I remember one crazy time I was lolling around in my back house. I say it was mine because my guy sort of gave it to me. He felt bad because they couldn't let me come in their house. I guess they thought I'd hurt Giggy or something, as if I'd ever have the nerve to go near her, claws or no. So because he was worried about what was going to happen to me come winter (like I'd never been through winter before!) my guy fixed up a spot in the little screened-in back house for me. I'd have pre-ferred a cardboard box at the end of the yard under some leaf litter but they gave me the back house. I said, "OK I'll take it." I'm a beggar after all.

So on this day I was lolling around on the table in my back house. I remember the day as being particularly bright, sunny, and with no wind. Giggy was tied up, hiding under the peony bush. Everything was pretty peaceful and what do you know, here comes Scarecrow sniffing around. I hadn't seen him in a while. My guy had put a bowl of dry for me out in the house and the Crow thought he'd help himself. I didn't par-ticularly care cuz I knew I'd get more eventually. Crow, on the other hand, never knew when he was going to get fed because his guy was a little crazy and not too regular with the food. Like I said, Crow was sure the skinniest cat ever. He was just too scared of everything to ever think about fighting over food. He was even too scared of people to ever make himself likable to somebody for a handout. Besides his crazy guy, Crow never really had anybody to feed him. He was perhaps the most pathet-ic creature in existence. When it rained on him, I always thought he looked like a skeleton. So I didn't mind him getting some of my dry. I like Crow. Besides I was just happy to be lolling around on that table falling in and out of nap land.

But peace was not to be had on this day. Just about the time Crow had gotten a mouthful down, my guy's girl took it in her head to come and check out the back house. When she opened the door, she saw Crow eating my food, and boy did she get mad! Poor Crow, startled out of a food eating reverie and then being afraid of any breathing thing on top of that couldn't do anything but freeze and stare, trying to sort through all sorts of panicky thoughts racing around in his head. Myself, I thought she was going to try and kill him because she kept shouting for him to "git." The sad part is that as she was standing there yelling at him to git, she was standing in the only place for him to git to. And of course Crow can't get closer than ten feet to any thing that breathes. I was kind of watching the whole thing in a stupor when I finally woke up completely and realized that if I didn't chase poor Crow out of there she was liable to hurt him. So I snarled at him and that might have been a mistake. Here was poor Crow: my guy's girl was snarling at him on one side. On the other side, his only ally in the world at the moment was snarling at him too and the only way out was blocked. The half-formed short-circuiting thoughts in his brain instantly coagulated into one big word that said "PANIC! PANIC!" He ran from one side of the little house to the other, back and forth, three, four times. He even climbed half-way up one of the screens. I imagine it would have continued on in this way if the girl hadn't finally gotten the good sense to get out of the way. I guess seeing Crow clawing his way up the wall made it somewhat obvious that he had no way out. So she finally stepped to the side holding the door open and Crow made a mad dash out of the house. Which direction did he go? You guessed it; smack dab into the peony bush where Miss Giggy, queen of all crabs, had just been roused from an afternoon nap. Twice as mean as she usually was, she snapped at Crow so hard he jumped straight in the air ten feet. He was already running when he landed on the ground and was out of sight in seconds. I laughed and laughed and Giggy even allowed a smile when she realized what happened. At least poor Crow got a few bites of food. After that Giggy got a little closer to me. Not real close, but closer. She definitely let me enter the kingdom at this stage.

Oh, I forgot to mention my name. One great day I was finally given a name. For eight entire lives and during my whole stay with the old lady I had never been given a name. A lot of things happened on my naming day. That was the day I entered the big house, the for-real big house. Giggy's house. My guy and his girl were busy that day, working in their garden. They had a small vegetable patch with tomatoes. I loved to run through the patch and hide. Not being particularly good gardeners, these people planted their tomatoes too close together, so when they grew into tall plants it was pretty dense underneath with just enough room to get through and see out a little. It was great; my favorite place in their yard. Well, on this day the girl was very excited because on their one squash plant a baby had just sprouted. They felt like proud parents and as I was rolling around in tomatoes I guess I got included in the excitement because they decided to name me after that squash right then and there. Cocuzelle. I thought it was a silly name and was really kind of let down that after all these years of not having a name I was going to be stuck with that thing. But because the word was so hard to say, they eventually shortened it and started to call me Gootsy. Now that was more like it. I liked that name, especially when she laughed and called me "Puss in Goots." Not being the type of cat that has been blessed with boots since I'm sort of gray and brown striped all over, I'd never been referred to as that cat of all cats, Puss in Boots, before. So the reference, inappropriate as it was, sort of made me feel proud.

It tickled me that I had an official name and a nick name on top, important-like. Later after Giggy and I had had our heart-to-heart she decided to bust my chops by telling me she had an official name too. OK, so my people always had official and nick names. I still felt important. Giggy was such a ball buster.

On my name day while all the excitement and gardening was going on, my guy and his girl put Giggy on her leash and propped the back door of the house open so they could go in and out easily. About late afternoon, they finally finished their work and went inside to watch TV. But they left the door propped open! And, naturally, I'm curious, so I wandered on in. Wow! The memories that came back to me when I hit that kitchen linoleum. There is nothing quite so comfortable to the paw as a nice smooth odoriferous kitchen linoleum. I could just see the old lady puttering around her tea pot and bread oven while I was half asleep on the register. Those were warm days and that linoleum brought it all back.

But that wasn't the half of it. There was so much more in that little house of theirs. Stuff I'd never seen before. Mainly boots covered all over with smelly mud and clothes stacked up every which where. I just followed my nose and went from one thing that caught my attention to the next. I made it into one room filled with the oddest looking items; weird, large round box-shaped, claw-busting leather things, strange table-like ironing boards that made funny sounds when you ran across them and what-not. Later, after I'd moved in, I found out that all those weird things made the most horrible sounds when held in the hands of my people and their friends. The first time I heard it I thought the end of the world was coming; Giggy just looked at me in disgust when I ran out of the room. It may well have been the only time in my life when I screeched. It was just that bad. Giggy told me not to worry, I'd get used to their practicing. She said maybe I'd learn to like it, their "music," as she called it. She said she learned and pointed out that it's the one time when the people seem to be really happy. She said I should try to sing along sometime. In Giggy's words, "Man, when she hits that high note, I just can't help myself, I have to join in!" Then it was my turn to be disgusted. As if I'd ever behave like a dog! Besides, compared to me, Giggy was a very vocal cat; I doubted if I'd ever feel the need to howl that way. It made my skin crawl.

On this day, however, I had no idea what was ahead and I was satisfied with smelling and seeing the house of my people. Eventually, I sniffed myself into the TV room, causing a minor ruckus that evolved into a "Well I guess it was inevitable." They put me outside and brought Giggy in with them and there I was left with that empty feeling. I was going to be watching Giggy through the window all night. She'd stare at me and I'd stare back and if I got too close, she'd spit so I'd have to step away.

I decided it was time to take matters into my own hands. That night after everyone was sleeping, I jumped to the window sill. There was just enough room for me to settle onto the ledge pressing myself against the screen. It was almost comfortable. The window was open and I thought I saw them on that most beautiful of human inventions: the bed. Well I was sick at heart for missing them or the old lady or something so I did what I never do: I cried. I don't vocalize much because I don't need to; I always help myself. All those lives spent in the street where I learned to avoid bad scenes taught me to get what I wanted without having to howl or complain or screech. I was surprised that I hadn't forgotten how to holler. When I saw that beautiful, warm, cozy bed I just sort of let loose with it. The two of them woke up I guess and looked at me for a moment through the window. I must have looked pretty pitiful because it didn't take long for them to get up and open the door. Boy was I happy. I was just about to head for the bed when a wall of smells hit me. I couldn't help it; I hadn't quite finished exploring before I got put out earlier and it was still all so new I didn't know which way to turn first. They watched me for a while and finally went to bed. I sniffed around a bit and even ran into Giggy in a corner who hissed and turned her head. I respectfully backed away and looked elsewhere. Finally I jumped up to the bed and fell into a sleep that I hadn't had for a year and a half. It was deep and pure: no dreams.

Needless to say, I was now in. I was allowed to come and go as I pleased. I devised a little grunt to get let out or in. It wasn't really a cry. I kept a wide space between me and Giggy, always giving her the right of way she required as the master of the house. I didn't have to do it so much after we'd had a heart-to-heart during which she told me about her childhood on a farm and then how she got her claws removed and had to stay inside all the time because of it. I was sort of sad for her. She'd never had any trouble in her life; she always had plenty to eat and was never caught by dogs or tortured by children. I mean she was thirteen years old and still on life number three. But even though she'd had an easy time of it, she hadn't caught a bird in ten years, hadn't chased the squirrels past the base of the tree, and in fact hadn't even climbed a tree since she was a kit. She still sharpened her claws once in a while out of habit, or maybe longing. Made me kind of like her even more. She was very regal even if her kingdom was pretty small. I resolved to never let her know I wasn't scared of her. I always crouched when she hissed as if at any moment she'd strike.

One thing I had a problem with was food. I loved it. Too much. By the time I was taking up residence in Giggy's house, I was eating regularly, but I was still somewhat hungry all the time. Well, my people had one of the best contraptions for a cat I'd ever seen. It was a never-ending cat food supplier! I found it during that first search through the house. It was a bowl with a sort of silo-looking attachment. As I ate and the level of food in the bowl dropped, more food from the silo fell into the bowl. The bowl was never empty! Sometimes some of the dry would get stuck and no more would fall, but I learned pretty fast to cram my paw up inside the bowl and knock some back down. I ate the whole silo-ful the first night. The next night I did the same thing. After the third night, the people got concerned and only filled up a bowl. It was a good thing too, I mean I was hungry but not that hungry. I just couldn't help it.

Giggy got fed once a day from a can and so I started getting that too. I didn't know what it was at first but after watching Giggy go for it, I didn't hesitate long. I preferred the dry but eventually the can caught on for me.

Giggy was funny with her food. She never minded me eating her food, but she couldn't eat with me around. I don't know why I did it, but when they put out our dishes of canned, I would never start to eat until Giggy showed me first and then I would wander over to her bowl and eat hers. She never spat or hissed, she just got somewhat bewildered and backed away. Finally the people got wise and fed her in a separate room with the door shut between us. She'd never eat all her food at once like me. I'd down the whole can and later, after the door was opened to let Giggy out, I'd find myself in the room finishing her share. Like I said I had a problem with food. I loved it too much. After a few weeks, Giggy started to look a bit like Scarecrow and I was getting mighty jolly.

About this time a very funny thing happened. You see, these people were stuck on the idea that I was a girl. One time when the Scarecrow and Socks came looking for me in the middle of the night my guy and his girl thought I was in heat. Crow and Socks were playing a joke on me howling and such outside the window and I guess it sort of looked like the ol' toms crying after Pumpkin. Well, that's what my people thought anyway. So when the day came to take me to the vet, I'll never forget the look on my guy's face when the Doc told him I was a boy. When we got home he ran to the phone and called his girl who was at work and said, "Guess what! My baby's not my baby; she's my good buddy!" Well that made him happy, and her too, I guess, cuz she said she'd never had a boy cat before. I had gotten so big by then I was actually starting to look like the tom that I was. I must say I was feeling pretty proud.

I have to say that life had never been better for me. I even liked the set-up more than the old lady's. What with Giggy and the garden and Socks and Crow and all the coons and skunks that lived in that neighborhood, there was always something going on; something to get into. And to top it all, I was never hungry anymore. I slept well anytime I wanted. No nasty toms or children ever bothered me. I even made peace with the cars I was so cocky. And that's when I made my big mistake.

On Tuesdays my guy and his girl were always going somewhere in their little red convertible. I liked that little car. When they left in that car, they'd be back soon. When they left in the big ugly gray van, they'd be gone for days. So as they were leaving on one regular Tuesday, I was feeling pretty good. I went and watched them go down the street in the middle of the road. And don't you know right as I was thinking how satisfied I was, licking my left paw and watching my guy and his girl in their little red car, Bam! Some big green thing comes speeding up behind me and in an instant there goes life number nine. I mean three short years representing the sum total of my nine lives up in a flick of a tail! My soul got shot all the way up to the top of the ugly van where I watched the whole scene. My head was crushed in immediately and fortunately I didn't feel a thing. The neighbor lady and her husband came out shaking their heads. They wrote a note and put it on my guy's door. Cars came and went and swerved around my carcass all day.

And then my people came home. They didn't see me because it was dark. But they read the note and came running back to the street. And oh boy! What a noise! Bawling and crying and saying my name over and over again. Jumping Jehosaphat! I'm a cat for pity's sake! You'd think I was the be all and end all or something.

But they were sweet. They wrapped me in a towel and dug a big hole for me in their backyard, which was great because now I get to stick around for awhile and watch things from up here before I dissolve. And man is the view great up here! I can see all the way over to the pet cemetery, and believe me that is one place I would never want to go! Just think of all them cats and dogs so close to each other, hissing and clawing all the time. Some of 'em just want to go to sleep but the rest of 'em keep everybody wide awake. Up here I can spook around for a while. The only other resident up here is my guy's mother. She told me she used to live in the house and she doesn't really want to leave because she's got to stick around and whisper things to him to make sure he doesn't make any mistakes. She doesn't really like me. She spends her time watching her son constantly putting that ol' fear in him whenever it's necessary.

One night I couldn't help myself, I had to let out an old-time howl. I guess I got to missing that bed too much. I was right above the window ledge I was on the night they let me in. I guess it was too much for me, I just let it rip. My guy came running out and looked around. I think I heard him sniff. His mother got mad at me and immediately started in: "You shouldn't have done that; that's not nice. He needs his sleep."

Oh well, I won't do it again. I'm beginning to fade anyway. It's probably time. But until I go all the way, I don't mind it up here. Even with his mother. I kind of like her. She loves my guy and so do I. Besides, she won't hate me for long. I'll break her down, just like I did with Giggy. I'm a lover, not a fighter.

THE BAD CAT

Richard Loller

We pulled into the driveway and there was the house we had lived in for twenty-five years. Thin green blades of alfalfa showed sparsely through the rotting straw in my vegetable garden. Sherry's flower beds were dark and bare. A few broken stalks still stood dripping in the cold February mist. The gray stone border was shiny with wet. A feeling of home welled in me. Two weeks in Mexico seemed like a sunny dream. We had seen and done a lot and now I was ready to be back home. I zapped the garage door and watched it slowly rise. Far in the back something large and orange moved. Then it was in the drive, skidding in the gravel and vanishing through the hedge.

"It's that wild tomcat. If he found the cat door to the garage he probably found the one to the house...DAMN!"

"If he did we'll smell it," Sherry said.

I pushed in the key as well as I could with a travel bag hanging from my wrist. Inside, I dropped the bag and punched in the alarm code. The smell was strong, hard to mistake. In the den it was stronger and there was a pile of cat crap on the couch. I looked out the picture windows across the shining wet deck to the river. The Cumberland was light brown and fast. The water was only a few feet below the backyard. The animals from the thickets along the river bank had moved up. We always had a surge of displaced mice in the winter. The cats got bored with killing them, but they would play with them for hours. I looked back down at the couch. There was another pile on the Persian rug under the coffee table.

"I'm going to kill him."

Sherry was looking behind the chair by the window. "There's more over here. Poop, that is. The pee is all over. And there are some clumps of hair that look like Cutie Pie's and Epie's. He beats up our cats."

"Not Butterball?"

"No. She's not afraid of him. He beats up Eppie and Cutie Pie if he catches them."

71

"He won't after I blow his head off."

"He's only a homeless cat. Scare him away."

"Hell, I tried. I damn near got him with a bottle rocket. But he was back the next day. That cat does not scare. And when we're gone he craps all over the house and beats up our cats to get even. I can end it. BANG!"

"You'll just have to catch him and take him somewhere."

"Shotgun shells are a lot less trouble and 100% certain."

When I woke up it was Saturday morning. We always try to come back on Friday so we'll have the weekend to rest up in.

I store scrap wood above the rafters in the garage. I climbed up and threw down some two by four's and some pieces of plywood. My idea was simple. A long box with a wood frame and sides of chicken wire. If he could see out on all sides he'd be more likely to go in. My hands were cold. I kept bending nails. The frame was heavy as a small piano. I had punctures and scratches on both hands from the chicken wire. I kept the edges outside. I didn't really hate the damn cat. He was just wild. He had to hustle to live. If it had stopped at food stealing I would have let it ride. But terrorizing my cats and crapping my house had to stop. I wanted him dead or far away.

I knew the perfect place. Across the river there were farms with cattle and crops. And in the river bottom there were woods, wide and wild. It was wild cat paradise.

The door came last. It was a solid square of plywood that would drop like a guillotine. When it was finished I stood up. It wasn't pretty. It was rough and out of square. But it was solid. It would hold any cat short of a lynx.

I rubbed my back and looked at it. My mind went back to a time when I was a boy and my daddy would build traps to catch the rabbits that raided our garden. His were long boxes made of four boards nailed at the edges. He closed up one end and rigged a dropping door like mine. The trigger was a stick with a notch cut in it. The stick went into a hole about the size of a quarter. There was a string from the trigger to the door. If a rabbit tried to get to the bait he would jostle the stick, the notch would slip, the stick would drop, the string would jerk, and the door would fall.

Daddy kept the rabbits he caught in a cage. He fed them rabbit pellets and vegetables from the garden. Mamma would cook them smothered in gravy for Sunday dinner. I can see those big brown gravy bubbles rising slowly in the black iron skillet. I can smell that delicious smell and almost taste it, now, remembering.

I tried to picture how the door was tripped, but I was only a boy then. I wanted to play, not help make rabbit traps.

I thought about my daddy and how he could make damn near

anything he needed, or fix anything he had to buy. I thought about his left hand with the missing finger joints, lost to a log chain somewhere in Guatemala. He was a self-taught Caterpillar tractor mechanic then, in the late 1930's, before I was born.

I remember Daddy with sadness sometimes. I wish I had tried to learn all the things he had to teach me, but I was too busy being independent, doing everything my way. I didn't think he had anything to teach me then. Now, I have to figure out things I could have learned so easily.

I studied the trap.

In the end I used a thin wire attached to a bag made from the foot of a pair of old panty hose. I filled it with dry cat food. The wire from the bag ran up through the chicken wire and forward to the door. I drilled a hole in the door and pushed a hairpin half-way through. It kept the door from dropping. The wire would pull the hairpin out when the cat pulled the bag. I tried it several times. It wasn't very certain. It was hard to pull out. Once it came partway out, stuck, and the door jammed halfway down.

This trap was not going to catch Mr. Devil Cat. He'd been around. If I botched the first try he'd never enter this trap again.

In the attic I found an old mouse trap with a dried mouse in it. I cleaned it up and tied it to the top of the trap Then I ran the wire from the bait to the trigger of the mouse trap. Another wire went to the jaws of the trap. Jaws? Anyway, it went from the part that whacks the mouse to the hairpin. When I barely touched the bait, the mouse trap snatched the hair pin out of the door. It popped me on the cheekbone an inch below my left eye the first time. I pictured myself blind in one eye. Mr. Safety First. The second and third tries I stood back. It worked perfectly. It had taken all day, but I had a good trap.

After dinner we blocked the cat door with books. I wanted our cats inside. The trap was heavy and awkward so I used a dolly to get it to the side of the house near the cat door. I figured he'd come back to see if he could still get in. When he couldn't he'd want the bait. That was the theory. I sprinkled a little cat food near the trap and went inside.

I woke up, listening. I thought I heard something, maybe a cat yowling. The clock said 4:23. I groaned and sat on the edge of the bed. God, I was sore. Getting old.

"What's wrong, darlin'?" Sherry whispered.

"Nothing. Go back to sleep." I pulled on some clothes. Quietly, listening, easing stiffly out the back door into the cold dark. Slowly. If he wasn't caught I didn't want to scare him off. I eased my head around the corner. I could dimly see the trap. Something moved. I heard a screech and the crash of cat against chicken wire. I pointed my flashlight. The big orange and white stripped tom lunged. There was red on his face. His big yellow eyes were bloodshot. The wire was bulged out . It looked O.K. I cut the light and backed slowly. No point in causing more cage bashing. I eased back into bed.

"Did we catch the cat?" Sherry yawned.

"He's in there."

"That's good," she murmured. I went to sleep.

The alarm buzzed at six. I got up and made a cup of coffee. It was still dark outside. After the coffee I got the dolly. Its rattling over the rough stone walk roused the cat. He crashed the bulging wire. In the pre-dawn light I saw him clearly. His face was flat and broad. There were scars there that were deeper and longer than the scratches from the wire. He hunched back into a corner, crouched, watching me with yellow eyes full of pain and hate.

"Well, old boy, you're not a pretty sight." I reached to pick up the cage. I jerked back as his paws hit the wire. Five little red circles dappled the gray stone walk. I licked the scratches and shook my head. Stupid.

Back in the garage I found gloves and an old green tarp. Once the trap was covered I got it onto the dolly. It was a struggle to fit it into the back of my wagon. A little flaw in the construction plan.

Across Briley Parkway bridge to East Nashville. Stopping to buy a bag of cat food at a rip-off market on Gallatin Road. Down Neeley's Bend until the houses gave way to farms. At the very end, below the farm land, was the new city park. It had a boat ramp and a large parking lot. As I pulled into the lot I saw it wasn't empty. On the far side an old man was sitting on the tailgate of a beat-up green pickup. I was nervous. I didn't want anyone to see me release the cat. The Neeley's Bend folks might not appreciate his little ways. I drove slowly over to the old man.

"How's it going?"

"Tolerable, son, tolerable. Running some worthless dogs. Times is they don't like to quit, you know. Reckon they'll drag they asses in 'fore long."

"Well, I imagine they will. Good luck."

I drove half way down the boat ramp, out of sight of the old man. The sun was a dazzling semi-circle above the dark cliffs across the river. It ricocheted from the burning silver and gold of the Cumberland and blazed blindingly into my eyes.

I stopped the car and got out. When the trap was down on the ramp and the tarp was off, I tore the top off the box of cat food and laid it on its side where he could see it. He hit the wire and yowled. I pulled up the door. The cat looked at the opening and froze.

"Get to hell and be gone, you old devil." But his orange tail was vanishing into the brush before the words were out. I loaded the trap into

74

the wagon.

I left the cat food. Something would eat it, maybe the coon dogs. Not him. I backed up the ramp and drove out of the lot. The old man waved. I felt fine. All the tension was gone. That old man wouldn't give a damn if I let loose a tiger.

The light reflecting from the river danced among the dark branches and dead leaves. Sparks from the melting frost flashed in the brown and green fields. Life was beautiful and full that cold morning. I though of my daddy, the cat with the bloody face, and breakfast.

A Resurrection To Remember

Frank Mann

Shame on me for feeling so smug and cocky after taking advantage of an old friend who was about to throw away an almost-new cane rocking chair. The only thing wrong with it was both rockers were cracked where they joined the base of the chair. If he couldn't fix it, well by golly I sure could. Just leave it to the well-trained son of a building contractor to replace those rockers in a jiffy and become the proud owner of a fine chair, tailor made for my newly constructed porch addition on my recently remodeled country home on the river. No Cracker Barrel restaurant in the country could offer finer porch accommodations.

Wouldn't my Dad enjoy rocking there while drinking in the gorgeous view. He was the one, even though mighty hard of hearing at eighty-nine, that still had that tremendous God-given talent in his fingers and brain that had allowed him to draw and design a lifetime of great buildings and projects. Our little remodeling project had been his most recent. With his typical diligence and push for perfection he had happily spent hours and hours sketching and planning with my wife, Mary Lee, eager to include in the plans her every whim and vision for what would become our retirement home. That effort seemed filled with an unusually strong love and devotion to the task. After all this was not any ordinary job. This one was for one of his kids. But this time that special enjoyment of one's own fruit of labor was not to be his. He died the very week the remodeling began, with me holding his hand, and Mary Lee close beside on the other side of the hospital bed.

My cockiness quickly evolved into humility when the nice young fellow at the wood-craft shop told me that rockers needed to be hewn from a tough hardwood such as white oak. The two pieces have to be at least two feet long and carved from a chunk of wood at least two inches by six inches thick in order to provide for the curvature of the rocker. To do it right would require a special type of band saw available in his shop (I didn't have one like that). And, oh yes, that piece of oak had been trucked in all the way from western Virginia. Cost? "Well-l-l-l, I'd say about a hundred dollars. But we won't charge you for the final sanding and staining. I'm sure you'll want to do that yourself." My response to the hundred dollars must have been a major unguarded expression of shock because that young fellow, forcing a smile and muttering under his breath at the same time, hiked quickly to a rack of short lumber pieces, chose my white oak, and headed for the band saw. Using the broken rocker I had brought along for a mold, he made short work of cutting a perfect pair of curved chair rockers, leaving only the sanding and staining to be done. "Give me thirty-five dollars, Mr. Mann, and promise not to tell my boss about this deal." I happened to know that he in fact was the boss. I gratefully gave him the cash, a big smile, a handshake, and was on my way.

So there I was. Rocking gently on our new porch, cat in lap, which was happily allowing me to simultaneously rub her pregnant tummy and rear section just ahead of the tail. She had come to really enjoy (and expect) this treatment, particularly in the final days as she swelled ever closer to delivery. The Halgrims, our good friends and former next door neighbors for the previous twenty-three years, had stopped out that Easter afternoon after supper, just to visit and enjoy the unbelievably beautiful sunset that was now a daily part of our lives in our new home. It was Robert Halgrim who had helped me put the finishing touches on the new porch deck barely two months ago. What a laugh we had that day when he pointed to Oppie under an oak tree hardly a hundred feet away, where she and a totally gray stranger of a tomcat were diligently going about the pleasant task of creating kittens.

Our heartiest guffaw came after the apparent climax of the brief affair, whereupon Oppie rose full height from her previously submissive crouched position, and gave the stranger a clean hard slap in the face signaling the fun was over. He took the hint. We've never seen him again.

Oppie adopted us a couple of months after we had moved into a 1950's vintage trailer, which had served as the caretaker's quarters for the fifteen acres we had bought. That leaky old piece of aluminum, together with a four-bay barn and the main house, made up the total of our retirement dream home purchase. We had planned to live in the trailer while I met the challenge of remodeling the main house. The previous owner had been a wealthy industrialist from Indiana who used to spend several weeks each year in this little Florida paradise. But in recent years, after his wife passed away, his visits became less frequent, and the property generally fell victim to pretty serious "deferred maintenance".

Why "Oppie?" you ask. Well, this classic alley rabbit, as my mother used to call these rather common spotted and striped, Sylvester the cartoon type felines, though always licking and preening as she would, still seemed to look disheveled no matter how hard she tried to pretty up. Kind of reminded me of the Oppie with Aunt Bea, Barney, and Andy that Mary Lee and I enjoyed in the sixties, shortly after we were married.

"Oppie, what IS the matter with you? Why don't you quit this squirming and turning around. I'm petting you exactly the same way I have for weeks now, and it always seemed to settle you down. What IS the matter? " Suddenly, with Oppie standing on all fours, still in my lap, I felt an unmistakable pool of warm wetness on my thigh. "Good Gosh Oppie, you've whizzed all over me!"

"No she hasn't Frank. Her water broke!" shrieked Caroline Halgrim, a mother three times and far more familiar with these matters than I.

Sure enough, bless her heart, the furry little adoptee that had stolen our hearts as the first permanent guest to our new home, barely a year old herself, was about to become a mother.

A veterinarian friend of mine had warned me that I only had a about sixty-two days from the time Robert and I had seen the gray visitor to get ready for Oppie's motherhood. On that advice I already had a good-sized cardboard box on the porch, sitting under the covered portion up against the kitchen wall. As gently as I could, I eased Oppie over to the box and carefully placed her inside it, with the top open. That most uncomfortable little lady had barely enough time to turn about two complete circles when she let out a blood-curdling yowl, fairly well frightening all four humans on the porch, and thereupon gave birth to her first baby. For some reason I made note of the time. It was 7:30 p.m., daylight savings. While the tiny baby was still wet I could see, nonetheless, that its coat was a combination of all the mother's colors, plus poppa's gray, woven in and out. A practical name for number one would have been Patches, but I chose right then and there to opt for Easter. And knowing cats usually have more than one kitten, I set aside Sunday, Resurrection and Calvary for the late arrivals, hoping I had enough names to go around. As it turned out we didn't need Calvary. Oppie's first litter would consist of three tiny, crying, quickly nursing, darling babies. And Oppie took to motherhood as though she had read a dozen books on maternity and regularly attended Lamaze classes in the weeks during pregnancy. I had seen quite a few animal births during my fifty-six years, but something about this almost-midwife experience with Oppie had me talking silently to God that night about the wonders of life and birth.

Sunday, arriving forty-two minutes after Easter, was pure gray from the fuzz on her nose to the tip of her tail. Absolutely no trace of any other color was to be found, that night or later. It also turned out that not only was her color exactly that of her daddy, so was her sex. It was several weeks later before I did a detailed check and learned that Sunday was indeed a "him."

Resurrection, the spitting color image of her mother, turned out to be the classic runt of the litter. Joining this world thirty minutes after her big brother, her days ahead would always see her coming in third in every possible way. Her older siblings always got the fattest nipple, and got it sooner. She could still bravely fight her way in for a snack each time the kittens' dinner bell was rung by Oppie, but she always appeared to come up short on the total grocery intake. None the less, she seemed to grow at a pace similar to the others. It was just that she started from so far back that she always looked a little pathetic, but oh so lovable.

The kittens were a good six weeks old, and I had overcome my concern about Resurrection's size and potential vulnerability. Of course their eyes were open by now, and Oppie had already moved them twice, as mothers will do to protect their young from predators. The last move however, had brought them back to the porch, albeit underneath, but only ten feet from where they were born. From their new residence we could watch them from inside the kitchen, playfully attacking each other and everything else on or about the porch. But just open the kitchen door, and all three disappeared instantly back underneath the porch.

One time, however, as I came out the door, anticipating the usual explosion of cats disappearing from the porch deck, Resurrection only walked toward the steps, slowly, as if struggling in great pain. She didn't even make an effort to run as I walked over and picked her up for the first time since the night she was born. She hissed, then cried, and tried to fight me all the while, but she seemed drained of any real strength. After several unsuccessful attempts to get her alone with Oppie for a really good meal, Mary Lee dug around and found a little eye dropper which we used to help feed the sick kitten. Oppie had tried hard to help her third baby, licking it constantly and lying down and wrapping her body around Resurrection's to make nursing easy. But the baby seemed to have either forgotten how to nurse or simply was too sickly to manage it.

I struggled with myself about whether to take the little one to the vet, opting finally to go first thing tomorrow morning if she wasn't better. I fixed another big box, laid it on its side, allowing Oppie and Resurrection to rest comfortably on a soft old towel Mary Lee had volunteered. I was encouraged when we saw Easter and Sunday join them about dark and settle in for the night. Early the next morning I rose to check on our beloved little family of kitties. When I looked in the box, Oppie, Sunday, and Easter were gone. Resurrection lay in a little furry ball, dead.

How in the world is it that human beings can get so terribly emotionally attached to dumb animals? Tears filled my eyes as I knelt and picked up that precious kitten. A horrible sense of guilt gripped me as I cursed myself for not taking the sick baby to the vet earlier. But suddenly, I found myself arguing with myself, using logic and reason, common sense, and maturity. "It's just a dadgum cat. A lot of people think nothing about putting a new, unwanted litter in a sack and throwing the whole kit and kaboodle in the river." But I was losing the argument. Too many other true life experiences kept flooding my thinking. Like the time our eleven month old beagle, Chainsaw, managed to slip out of the house while we were all gone and get himself killed on the nearby street. It had been Caroline Halgrim that had to call me at work and tell me that some nice man had just brought the puppy to my home and laid it in the carport after it had been hit. She couldn't bring herself to tell me it was dead, only saying he was hurt real bad and I needed to come home. She and Robert had watched us raise that little dog, indeed helped us raise that little dog. They loved it too.

That time I had just wrapped the lifeless creature in an old blanket and had gone inside to the utility room to get a shovel when Robert showed up. Caroline had called him at work too. He just walked into our house, without knocking as my close friend and neighbor had done for years. We came face to face in the long hallway, two full grown, macho men, not really knowing what to say to each other, tears flowing profusely down both faces. At times like that I guess true friends really don't have to say anything. Just being there speaks all the words you need.

I wanted to get Chainsaw buried before the boys came home from school. They were eight and eleven, and they loved that little dog, as only youngsters can, their first-ever pet. Robert helped me. I managed to put up a little cross before my first boy got there. Holding him as tightly as I could without hurting him, I told him about Chainsaw. And we cried and cried. Then I went through it all again when his brother got home. The three of us only thought we had finally gotten a hold on ourselves when their mommy got home. That became the saddest scene of all. Four loving people, very much in pain.

As I dug the little grave site for Resurrection, I found my mind returning to the final hours in my Dad's life. He hadn't been gone yet for even a year and memories of his life, and particularly his last hours, were still light-bulb bright in my mind. My mother and brother and I and our families had been tending Dad's bedside all day long, giving him sips of water and checking on the seemingly endless bundle of wires and tubes that protrude virtually everywhere when you've suffered a heart attack. Mary Lee and I were by his side when he spoke his very last words. Eyes closed, but with a clarity far beyond that of earlier hours as his strength had steadily declined, Dad exclaimed to us - or perhaps only in amazement to himself - "It's like a whole new world."

Stunned, I looked at Mary Lee for confirmation of what I was sure I had just heard. Quietly, she said those exact words.

There will never be a doubt in my mind that my father's last words in this world were his first words to those gathered to greet him in his new one. Three hours later his tired old heart recorded its last beat on the hospital monitor. And yes, we all cried again. A lot. But for me I am not able to say now where the tears of pain stopped and the tears of joy began. For I cannot think of my father's life without feeling the most profound sense of gratitude to that unseen divinity who willed that I should be George Mann's child and grow to manhood under his influence.

The name "Resurrection" began to take on a much broader meaning as I finished covering the simple grave with the patch of weedless sod I had carefully saved. And that Easter, on which we celebrated His resurrection in the morning and the kittens' birth in the evening, now takes on special meaning too, as I think back on it, so full of joyous events that ultimately joined so many beautiful thoughts, people, and happenings. Together they remind me, and will over and over again each new day I awake - What a wonderful thing is this marvelous experience and opportunity called Life.

It had taken a little kitten that ever so briefly passed my way to help me realize what great joys I've really been able to experience for so many years through precious friends and family members.

Yes sir. What a wonderful Easter! And what a true Resurrection!

XENA RULES

Leslie C. McCarthy

A faint fluttering started in my stomach as my receptionist brought the last client of the day, my secret passion, to my office.

"Ben, how nice to see you again. Coffee?" I asked as I gestured for him to sit down.

Disposing of the preliminaries, we got down to the business of tax planning for Ben's flourishing dental practice, addressing each item on my list in turn - deductible expenses, health insurance for employees,

Keogh accounts, profit-sharing, the benefits of becoming a corporation. We were almost through when, to my horror, the fluttering in my stomach that I had assumed was caused by my unspoken (and apparently unreturned) attraction to my client turned into a very audible growl, not unlike the one my cat makes when displeased about something, and I realized that I had neglected to eat lunch yet again.

Every time I got near that man, something embarrassing happened to me. First, on my way to greet him in the waiting room on his initial visit, I caught my heel in the carpet, reeled drunkenly through the doorway, and ended up clutching wildly at him to keep myself from falling. Generally viewed as a suave business woman, at our next meeting I put the entire staff into hysterics by leaving the ladies room, sweeping through the waiting room giving gracious smiles to the clients, and going on to my office, all blissfully unaware that I had my skirt tucked into my pantyhose. How I was able to face him after that, I'll never know.

"It's getting late and it sounds like you could do with something to eat," Ben said with a sympathetic smile. "Join me for dinner?"

Kismet must be making up for all the disasters by giving me this chance with the man of my dreams, I thought.

Lingering over coffee after a wonderful dinner, we got to know each other a little better. Marathons are his favorite sport, whereas mine is sunbathing with a book in hand. Navy blue is his favorite color, mine is fuchsia. Othello is his favorite play, but I detest Shakespeare. Parachuting out of a plane is something Ben has always wanted to do, while I suffer from a fear of heights. Quebec is his favorite place to visit, but he doesn't think they should secede from the rest of Canada. Reflecting on the fact that I like anywhere that is hot, has sand and salt water, and I couldn't care less about their politics as long as I could take my cat with me, I realized that we really didn't have a lot in common. Still, that just made him even more attractive, and the feeling seemed to be mutual. The opposites-attract bit I suppose.

Under a full moon (Kismet again) we strolled back to my apartment and I invited Ben up for a second cup of coffee. Vowing that nothing would give him greater pleasure, he followed me in.

While the coffee was brewing, I anxiously awaited my cat's decision on whether or not I could continue to see him.

Xena shot out from under a chair and sank her claws into Ben's rear end as he was bending over to scan the titles in the low bookcase, then disappeared from view as he leaped up with an outraged howl, hands clutching his injured backside. Yielding to her unmistakable rejection of him as a regular visitor to our home, I reluctantly escorted Ben to the door, muttering apologies. Zero hour with Xena, attack cat, has once again left me without a date.

Not Yet

L. C. Mohr

She glanced at her watch. The bus was two minutes late, which wasn't late at all really, considering its usual bad service. She'd left herself an extra hour--she always did when she had a doctor's appointment.

She used to take a cab but she'd stopped doing that. It wasn't the money. She could easily afford the expense, but the drivers always made her nervous. They either drove too close to the car in front or took the wrong turns, and then got angry at her because she didn't know how to direct them. After all, she'd never driven a car. How was she supposed to know which highways to take?

She eased her tote bag off her shoulder -- it was creasing the fur of her mink jacket -- and rested it on the cracked wooden bench. It was safe enough there. Most of the commuters from her neighborhood caught earlier buses. She was alone. She paced in front of the bench, then checked her watch again. She sighed; still no bus.

Suddenly, she jumped at a noise behind her -- a soft noise, like an animal. She looked around, glancing under the bench. It had sounded like a cat meowing. No, nothing there.

The sky was starting to cloud up. She took a deep breath and glanced at her watch again. She looked up. Oh good, she thought, here it comes.

It was moving too fast, as usual. It must be that driver -- the one who always frightened her, the one who pretended he wasn't going to stop at all. Then he'd slam the brakes on and skid to a stop with a bone-rattling screech. Always in the middle of the street -- not near the curb where he should be. He made her feel that he resented having to stop for her.

She turned toward the bench and reached out for her bag. The strap caught between two of the slats. She tugged it. It tightened. She pulled it again, then glanced back toward the bus. It was almost here.

She grabbed her bag and yanked hard. It wouldn't budge.

The bus screeched to a stop in the middle of the street. She looked at it. Looked back at the bench, tugged again. Looked at the bus again. The driver glared out the open door at her. She looked up at him, back at the bench, up at him -- she felt tears pricking her eyes.

The driver made a noise like a growl, snapped the doors shut, and pulled away.

She realized she'd been holding her breath and exhaled. She turned back to the bench and pulled the straps one last time. The bag came loose. She grabbed it, flung it over her shoulder, and looked toward the bus. But it was a block away already. Should she run -- try to catch it?

As she stared after the fast-receding bus, a yellow puff came out the back. Then a flame.

The bus was on fire!

She watched in open-mouthed horror as flames crept up the sides of the bus like giant orange hands. The bus made a turn and was out of her sight. Then she heard an enormous bang and screams!

She let her breath out, clutched her bag with white knuckles and stood paralyzed. She heard sirens. She turned slowly and started back toward her house. It was only a block and a half but her knees trembled the whole way. As she stepped onto the front stair and fumbled for her key, she heard a mewing noise and jumped back.

There was a cat sitting on her front porch. It was several shades of orange and brown, the kind people referred to as a calico, she thought. But she didn't know much about cats. It was licking its paw, but its actions seemed strange. Then she realized that the cat was hurt. It was holding its paw up in the air staring pitifully at her, meowing. She approached it gingerly. It sat very still, as though waiting for her.

She surprised herself by leaning down and picking it up. It meowed gently and fitted itself comfortably into the crook of her arm. She found her key and let herself into the house.

I guess I'm not going anywhere after all, she thought. She called the doctor's office, told his nurse she'd missed the bus and made an appointment for the following week. She didn't want to tell her what had really happened. But she'd tell Jack.

Ah, Jack! She still smiled every time she thought of him. He was so tall and so handsome. With his silver hair and sparkling blue eyes, Jack was the most elegant man she had ever seen. And he had noticed her! He had seen her shopping at the supermarket and had come over to talk to her. He had noticed her there before, he'd said. She couldn't get over the wonderfulness of a man like Jack wanting to be with her. Actually being attracted to her! Jack was coming to take her to dinner tonight. She would tell him all about it. He would make sense of it all.

She heard a noise and looked down. It was the cat. She'd almost forgotten about the cat. The poor thing must be hungry. She thought about giving it some milk, but she vaguely remembered reading some-where that milk wasn't good for cats, so she put out a bowl of water and opened a can of tuna for it. It daintily but quickly swallowed half the food, then looked up at her and smiled. She laughed at herself. Cats couldn't smile. But this one seemed to.

She spent most of the afternoon sitting on the couch with the cat on her lap. She felt soothed and happy. The cat was so soft -- and clean. That was something she'd worried about but she needn't have. Also the cat's paw seemed to have healed.

The doorbell rang. She jumped and the cat leaped gently to the floor. She glanced at the clock. Oh my, it was after six. She must have fallen asleep! She rushed to the front door, smoothing her hair.

"I must look a mess," she said when Jack's smile turned to a quizzical frown.

"No, no," he protested in that deep melodic voice she loved so much. "You look wonderful." He leaned down and pecked at her cheek.

Suddenly she saw him freeze and his face paled.

"What is that?" he growled in a voice she didn't recognize.

She turned. "Oh, it's just a cat I found..."

"A cat?" He glared at her. "How dare you! I hate cats!"

She shook her head. "No, I don't know. I didn't think..."

"You never think! You're a fool! I despise cats!" He was screaming now. "Do you think I would put up with you if I knew you were going to collect CATS?!" He spat the word at her. "Even your money doesn't make it worth ..."

She stared at him. "My money?" she whispered.

He was panting and his face had turned bright red. Without another word he turned and left the house, slamming the door behind him.

She stared at the closed door for a moment. Then she heard a noise. She looked down. The cat sat at her feet, licking its paw. It looked up at her and smiled. A sad smile this time, but still a smile. Suddenly the cat's smile turned to a frown and it meowed loudly. It walked to the door and scratched once with its paw. She continued to stare at it.

"You want to go out?" She opened the door. The cat took a step out, sat on the front porch and turned its head back to look at her. It meowed again, as though calling her.

"What is it? It's dark out. I don't want to come out."

But still the cat meowed at her.

"No -- you go do what you have to do and I'll wait here."

The cat held up its paw and meowed pitifully.

"Oh, all right." She took a step out onto the porch. Then she saw it. Smoke coming from the side of the house. "What..."

The leaves she'd piled there yesterday were smoldering. She ran to the other side of the house and pulled on the hose. Meanwhile she could smell the burning leaves. Just as she realized the hose was hopelessly tangled, she remembered that she had shut the water off yesterday when she'd finished raking. She ran back to the smoldering pile. She could see flames now. She glanced next door. There was a hose!

As she started to force her way through the rose bushes that grew along the property line, a man came out the side door. "What is it?"

"Fire! There's a fire and it's right against my house!"

The man grabbed the hose, pulled it through the bushes, and doused the burning leaves. Gray bitter smoke filled the air. He turned to her.

"Good thing you saw it. There's a lot of wood in that crawl space and the fire could easily have worked its way up through your floor ." He smiled at her--a smoky, dusty smile.

She smiled back. "Thank you so much."

He pulled a large red handkerchief from his pocket and wiped the grime off his face. "Not the nicest way to meet somebody, but..." He held his hand out. "I'm Henry."

"Grace," she said, shaking his big warm hand.

"And what's her name?" He asked, looking down.

"Who? Oh!" The cat looked up at the two of them. Grace smiled. "I don't know yet. I don't even know if it's... I mean if she's mine. I just found her this morning. Actually ... she's the one who found the fire."

"Well," he grinned. "I always said cats were smarter than humans. Say..." he began, then hesitated. "I was just going out for a lonely bachelor dinner. How about joining me?"

"Well..." She had plans for this evening, didn't she? Oh, no, she almost forgot... there was no more Jack in her life. She smiled shyly back. Why not? She nodded. "I'd like that."

The paper boy flung the Gazette onto the porch, next to the other three untouched newspapers. It unfurled and lay face up, gently rustling in the early morning breeze. A calico cat, who was sleeping on one of the older papers, opened an eye, got up and stretched slowly. She began to delicately lick her paw. As the first rain drop fell on her head, she glanced up, frowned softly and padded away, leaving the headline visible:

THIRD WOMAN KILLED BY "RED HANDKERCHIEF" STRANGLER

LOVEY

Betty Newsom

One summer my husband and I and our four children camped in our fold-down canvas-top camper in my parents backyard for a few days. My mother warned me to keep my children away from a stray calico kitten because it was limping and she was afraid it might be sick.

We placed our fold-out camper under an old apple tree next to my great grandparents's antique barn. The next morning we discovered that the little calico kitten, who limped and might be sick, had managed to climb up on the camper step, jump several inches up the metal side of the camper, wriggle under the snapped-down canvas wall, jump up and curl up in bed beside three-year-old Kenny.

My husband and I carefully looked her over and decided she wasn't sick but just had a sore leg. Every night the small kitten found a way to climb into the camper and sleep next to Kenny. When we returned home we took her with us.

I don't like to give a new animal a name until I'm sure it's not going to wander off, so some time went by before the little calico kitten received her name. One day, while I was folding clothes, I was thinking about a name for her and thought we might call her Lovey. Later that day, since the kitten had adopted Kenny, I asked him what he thought we should name her. I was surprised and pleased when he said "Lovey."

Of course, that became her name.

Lovey was a lot of company for Kenny when the older children went back to school. One afternoon, when she was almost full size, I looked out in the front yard and realized that there was something unusual about her that day--something quite different. Kenny had taken eight Band-Aids and stuck them all over her fur coat.

I didn't know what might happen if Lovey tried to lick or scratch them off. I wasn't brave enough to go outside and start ripping Band-Aids off a cat, so before she could start trying to pick at them herself, I took my scissors outside and cut the hair underneath each Band-Aid and lifted them off. She went around looking like an awful "bad hair day" until all of her fur grew out to the same length again.

One day when I was alone in the house I heard a terrible commotion out in the garage. When I investigated the noise, I found Lovey howling and jumping around trying to kill a fishing rod. Every time she jumped or hit it the rod would slam against the wall. She must have tried to play with the fishing lure on the end of the line and it had stuck in the bottom of her paw.

There are a lot of things that I wouldn't volunteer to do. Tackling an outraged cat, in severe pain, to remove a three-barbed fishing hook from her paw is high on my things-I-really-don't-want-to-do list. However, since I was the only person at home, it automatically became my job.

I wrestled Lovey into a bath towel with only her head and the harpooned paw sticking out. I placed her on the washer in her terry-cloth strait jacket. Talking very sweetly and confidently to her, I pried the hook out of her foot. She licked the paw clean and it didn't become infected. That evening I delivered a stern lecture to the boys about removing all lures and fish hooks from their lines before they put their fishing poles away.

A few years later we built a new house in my great-grandfather's woods, across the field behind my parents' home.

Our calico cat, Lovey, had returned to her place of birth, but it wasn't an easy journey for her or for me.

The day she returned to her birthplace I fastened her in a box in the back seat of my station wagon. As I was driving down the road she clawed her way out of the box and, terrified, agitated, and howling, she started bouncing off the seats and windows trying to escape. I drove very slowly the last five miles of the ten-mile ordeal, with Lovey clinging to the back of my seat, her front claws embedded in my neck and shoulders.

When we arrived at the woods I put her in a wire chicken pen under a big tree. She lived in the pen for three days until she calmed down. When she realized that all of our family was staying in this place and that this was now her home as well, we set her free. She was fine after that.

Time passed and Lovey became a mother.

Our new house had a cement patio just outside the dining room door, and the dryer vent blew warm air out across it. During the cold months, Lovey and her kittens gathered at that corner of the patio and let the warm air blow over them. Even after the dryer had shut off, they would huddle together on top of the warm spot of cement.

It was a good arrangement for the adult cats, but unfortunately the little kittens liked it, too. When the dryer was off, the kittens liked to crawl into the four inch aluminum exhaust pipe. As they grew bigger, they could no longer turn around to crawl out so they had to back out. They looked funny scooting out of the dryer vent backwards, decorated with lint fuzz.

I became concerned that some of them would get stuck in the pipe and we wouldn't be able to rescue them, so we placed a wire cover over the vent. That allowed the warm air to escape and eliminated the possibility of our kittens suffocating inside the narrow pipe, and it still allowed the cats their sauna-like experience on the patio.

Most cats seem to be instinctively drawn to dark, narrow places. We had a large stack of firewood by the barn that the kittens liked to climb on. When they were little they could crawl into some of the spaces between the chunks of wood to hide and take naps. As they grew bigger, they would sit and stare at the woodpile. They seemed to be trying to figure out why they could no longer jump into their kittenhood hiding places. The woodpile still looked the same as it always had to them. They just didn't realize they had outgrown the small cozy spaces.

Most of Lovey's kittens grew up at our home in the woods. At one time I counted seventeen cats on the place, even though we were very generous in sharing them with our family and friends or a rumored friend of a friend's friend.

Before Lovey's next-to-last bunch of kittens arrived, she became bigger and bigger until she looked like she had swallowed a soccer ball. When she finally gave birth there were eight kittens. Four were calico-colored like Lovey and the other four were a variety of colors.

When all of them tried to eat at the same time, the bigger ones would crowd out the smaller ones. While Lovey was out on a hunting trip, we fixed a second box and put the four calico kittens in it. When she came back inside the garage/family room, she carefully looked over the new housing arrangements and accepted the two-box system. After that she divided her time between the two boxes. We referred to one box as the "Calico Room" and the other as the "Nursing Home."

The eight kittens must have worn her out. Her last litter was only two babies. When they were about three-weeks old, I left for church one afternoon driving our pickup. I stopped at a restaurant thirty-five miles from home and when I opened the truck door, something fell out onto the parking lot. It was one of the little kittens! When I put it back in the truck, I found the other one behind the seat. Our pickup had been parked out by the trash barrel that afternoon, and Lovey must have moved them in when the doors were left open.

I was thirty-five miles from home, and still twenty miles away from church. I wouldn't be going back home for several hours and faced a whole evening trying to care for two tiny nursing kittens that barely had their eyes open. I went on to church and while I was there, I spooned some diluted milk into their mouths several times. When I returned home, Lovey was sitting in the driveway looking for the mobile home she had moved her family into. She was glad to see me coming down our road and turn into the driveway.

After that episode, we were careful about keeping all vehicle windows rolled up and the doors closed. Even then, while the kittens were still small enough for her to carry around, I always checked behind the seat before I left home.

We never learned what finally became of Lovey. When she failed to show up to eat we searched for her but couldn't find her. We lived in a thick woods in the country, surrounded by farmland. She enjoyed complete freedom to wander around, as I don't like to keep animals cooped-up inside of a building. One summer day she had unexpectedly limped into our lives and twelve summers later she simply walked out.

Lovey has her special place in our hearts. She was a member of our family and she can never be replaced.

AHOY MATE!

Janice K. Payne

She was a wild little kitten. She could stay out all night and sleep all day. She was free to climb trees, roll in the grass and chase birds. She didn't need to rely on humans to take care of her...or did she?

Her name is now Pinto. As her owners, we were not permitted to touch her for the first four months of her life. The first time I picked her up, she clearly let me know that she wasn't going to put up with that. She was born under an apartment building and was promptly abandoned by her wayward mother. A large male cat named Slug took her under his wing and showed her the best eating-places, how to stay dry in the rain and where to hide from those humans.

One of the best eating-places was at the top of the staircase leading to an apartment my husband and I were renting. I had just lost two older cats and I had begun to feed several strays in the neighborhood. One night we discovered we were also feeding the neighborhood possums.

"If we don't have any cats, why are we still buying cat food?" my husband would ask with a twinkle in his eye. My neighbors would also leave bags of cat food on my doorstep. I became the neighborhood cat lady. Each day when I returned home from work, six stray cats would greet me in the driveway to let me know it was dinnertime.

Every night Pinto would bounce up the staircase with Slug to see what was for dinner. Eventually Pinto mustered up the courage to venture into the apartment where she discovered the soft furry afghan that I had draped inside a cardboard box. Of course the afghan was for her.

She would jump into the box and fall asleep immediately. One night I couldn't bear to wake her from an evening nap to send her out the door so I decided it was time to buy a litter box and allow her to sleep over. After sleeping over many nights, we felt it was our duty to get her vaccinated and spayed. She became ours at that moment.

Two months later my husband and I moved back on to our 31-foot sailboat and decided to move Pinto too. Her life has never been the same.

I showered her with cat toys to keep her entertained and her favorite toy of all was a large rubber eyedropper bulb. We would throw the rubber bulb the length of the boat and as it bounced wildly about, she would chase after it. Pinto is very intelligent and she quickly figured out that for the game to continue she would need to return the rubber bulb to us so that we could throw it again. She merely picked up the bulb in her mouth, ran back to us and dropped it in front of us. When the game is her idea, she merely finds the toy and brings it to us. I had never seen a cat play fetch.

Pinto has adjusted to life on the boat quite well. She has investigated every inch of the boat from the anchor locker in the bow to the engine compartment in the stern. She uses her claws to open all of our lockers. Oftentimes when my husband returns from work, the locker where we keep Pinto's food is wide open with the contents spilled onto the berth. Pinto has been digging for her dinner.

On the boat, Pinto is able to play outdoors without risk of encountering cars, fleas or other animals. She watches birds, rolls in the sun, chases bees and has even captured a few crabs. We believe the lifestyle agrees with her.

After a few months of having her onboard, my husband decided that Pinto should experience a ride in our dinghy. "But cats don't like water," I kept telling him.

"She needs to get used to riding in a dinghy. What if we are at anchor and have to take her ashore to the vet. She might like the dinghy," he said.

"Yeah sure," I mumbled under my breath.

I agreed and the first day the three of us rode around in the dinghy. Pinto was crouched under the seat only peeking out occasionally to see how she could escape from this ride of terror. The next day my husband decided that Pinto needed another dinghy ride. I chose to stay behind on the boat to do some chores. The only problem was that Pinto could see that I was staying behind. I'm sure she was wondering why she had to suffer through this dinghy ride if I was permitted to stay behind. My husband motored about twenty feet away from our dock and as I watched I could tell Pinto was going to jump. I signaled for my husband to come back and sure enough as he was heading for the dock, Pinto dove out of the dinghy. I jumped to the dock and stood in horror as Pinto swam to the dock. Indeed I had never seen a cat swim. As she reached the dock, I pulled her out of the water by the scruff of the neck. We then gave her a bath, dried her off and all was well. She now had eight lives remaining.

Pinto has always been curious and she developed a tendency to go exploring. We knew having her wander the docks was unacceptable so we trained her to stay aboard the boat by aiming a squirt bottle of water at her when she jumped off. We also put a harness on her and occasionally attached her harness to a leash we had secured on deck. With the leash, she had about 10 feet of line to wander around the boat. One day my husband and I were down below and we noticed things on deck seemed quiet. Then we heard a dull thump. I decided to poke my head out the hatch and check on Pinto. She was nowhere. All I could see was her leash going over the side of the boat. I jumped out into the cockpit and looked overboard and there she was in the water paddling away. I couldn't reach her so all I was left to do was reel her in by the leash. Only Pinto knows what really happened that day. Perhaps she was chasing a sea gull and misjudged the edge of the boat. She was down to seven lives and counting.

On another occasion my husband and I were traveling up the coast of California and we stopped for a few days in a marina. Pinto went outside to investigate and unbeknownst to us, she made a jump over to our neighbor's boat. A few minutes later we began looking for her and couldn't find her anywhere. I finally heard a tiny meow and saw her big black eyes inside the porthole next door. I panicked when I realized my neighbor's boat was all locked up and I had no way to get to Pinto. How were we going to explain to our neighbor that our cat was now locked inside his boat? I climbed inside our dinghy and pushed myself over to the porthole where she was. It was now time to coax her out. I had her favorite toy and a jar of baby food I was using to entice her.

Just at that moment our other neighbors came down to their boat. They gave me a sideways look trying to figure out what I was doing standing in our dinghy.

"Oh, you must be cleaning today too," the woman said. "We have a full day of cleaning to do ourselves."

"Yes, I'm just cleaning," I said. At that moment I was wondering if they noticed I had absolutely no cleaning supplies with me in the dinghy. My husband wandered over to talk to the neighbors and I went back to my coaxing. I finally got Pinto's head far enough out the porthole for me to grab her by the scruff of the neck. I quickly put her back on our boat and she ran around and greeted my husband. He was quite surprised and relieved to see her.

One episode not long ago was perhaps the scariest for all of us. It was a Saturday afternoon and Pinto had gone outside on deck. She was not leashed, but we were checking on her every couple of minutes. At one point she had vanished. My husband and I began searching the docks horrified that she had gotten into someone else's boat or perhaps had fallen overboard. There was no sign of her for over two hours. My husband was riding around in our dinghy searching for her in the water. I was walking the dock calling for her. We imagined her in someone else's boat as they cast off to head for Hawaii. What an adventure that would be. I finally remembered a story that my husband had told me about cats getting on top of the fiberglass floats under the docks. I laid down on the dock by our boat and with my head almost in the water, I looked up under the dock. I began calling Pinto's name and at first I thought I heard a tiny meow. I didn't believe it so I continued calling. Pinto's meow got louder as she realized we were looking for her. I traced her meow down the dock a little way and there she was, sitting on top of the float under the dock. She was drenched and shaking like a leaf. I ran to get my husband and the two of us laid on the dock. We had to grab her and dunk her back in the water to pull her out around the dock. When she realized we were there to help she got very still and allowed us to give her a bath and take her home. Again, only Pinto knows what really happened that day.

We've had Pinto for four years now and we've cherished every moment. She is a very dear sweet animal with lots of energy. I'm not sure how many lives she has left but we've all learned a lot about life aboard a sailboat with a lively cat.

THREE CAT STORIES

Craig Osborne Snow

Gramps, The Tree, And The Cat

Gramps for the most part was pretty smart but I remember one time when he slipped up a little. He had some poplars growing between the house and the chicken yard and decided he wanted to do some serious pruning. With the aid of a ladder, he climbed twenty feet up one of the trees and started sawing away on a big limb. When he couldn't get a good angle, he climbed out on the limb. His plan was to saw part way through and then get back on the ladder to finish the job.

Gramps didn't bounce worth beans when the limb broke off. Busted several ribs when he landed. Even spent a couple of days in the hospital telling them he wanted to go home. The doctor let him out on condition he would stay a few days with us resting. He didn't like it but he agreed.

Now, we had an old red velvet padded rocker with open arms that was really comfortable. That was where Gramps headed like a homing pigeon. But Gramps had no more than gotten settled when Tiger, our silver tabby cat, sat down in front of him and started a stare-down contest. You see, the red rocker was also Tiger's favorite chair. Tiger was the king of the roost. He was not used to having competition for what was naturally his. After about fifteen minutes, Gramps asked what was the matter with our cat. I told him that Tiger usually took his naps in the red rocker and he wanted his chair.

Gramps never said a word, just chuckled and proceeded to ignore Tiger. That was a mistake. After a few minutes, Tiger went to stage two. He got up and padded around toward the back of the chair and off to one side where he had a good view of Gramps' flank. Then ever so carefully he unsheathed one claw and sank it to the hilt in Gramps' rump.

Broken ribs and all, Gramps came out of that chair like a spring chicken. He turned around and in the chair staring up at him was Tiger.

Gramps grinned and went over and sat down on the couch. It seems like he had gotten a little smarter since falling out of the tree.

More Than A Furry Friend

I never realized what I had until I almost lost it from sheer stupidity. But to explain my blunder I have to tell you a little bit about Marco and what made him so special.

Marco, although smart, was not the brightest cat I have known, nor the biggest (though he was the longest). He was your typical run-of-the-mill silver tabby, a bit on the lean side, always inquisitive (but not obnoxiously so).

Marco was also the most gentle cat I have ever known. Generally cats, if you get in their face, will let you have a taste of claw to say the least. Marco from day one never drew blood intentionally unless you happened to be a mouse, a bird or a dog. The first two he would eat; dogs were creatures he more or less tolerated.

To give an example of Marco's grace under fire, one time when he was about four years old my cousin Carol came out with her daughters when they were at the doll-playing stage. The girls got hold of a dress my mother had made for the youngest of them and put Marco in it. He was not happy but he put up with it until the littlest one decided to see if his eyes were removable. She was gouging and probing his eyes with her stubby, fat little fingers. Marco rolled his head from side to side and began meowing stridently for help. But never once did he try to claw or bite. All he wanted was for me to come to his rescue, which I did.

Marco also wouldn't roughhouse with the other cats. If they attacked his tail he would pull it in or walk away.

When Marco was about five I got a burr under my saddle and decided to try to get him to fight like the rest of the cats. I gave him a good old fashioned tummy-tickling teasing, the kind where, if you aren't fast enough, you would usually expect to pull back a bloody stump. But Marco wouldn't fight no matter what I did. I must have tried for almost an hour but still he wouldn't retaliate.

When I finally stopped he got the saddest look on his face and went outside. When he came in to eat a few hours later I went over to pick him up and he walked away from me. I reached to pet him and he evaded me and went towards the living room. He stopped in the doorway and looked back at me as though I were a stranger. Again I tried to pet him, but he avoided any contact. I got him cheese (his favorite snack food) and he wouldn't touch it. He turned up his nose and went back outside.

After three days of being totally shunned, I couldn't take it any more. I felt as if I had lost my best friend. That evening, I grabbed Marco while he was eating and took him up to my bedroom and shut the door. And this time for over an hour I held him and petted him and told him how much I loved him and that I was so sorry for what I had done. I cried and told him I wanted things the way they were before.

I was sitting on the bed with my back up against the headboard. I let him go. He stepped away and looked at me for the longest time (it seemed like forever) and then he came back over and lay down beside me and went to sleep. Neither of us ever brought the subject up again.

The Dowager Queen

The other day I got to remembering how when I used to help Gramps feed the dairy cows they would always queue up in the same order. Things got vicious if one of the cows tried to take her turn ahead of time. The head gal was downright mean. One old cow at the bottom of the pecking order had an abscessed jaw. I felt sorry for her and sometimes when I was putting out the feed I would shoo the other cows away until she had eaten. I did her no favors. The queen would be twice as nasty to her later.

Then there was Queen Cleo the cat.

94

Of course, Cleo didn't start out queen of anything. She was a smallish calico who as a kitten showed no potential at all. The first year we only kept her because we couldn't give her back.

Cleo didn't seem to know which end was up. To give you an idea, one time she climbed about twenty feet up one of the trees and then couldn't figure out how to come down. She finally decided to come down head first, so of course she fell and lit on her side. Couldn't even land on her feet.

A couple months later Cleo happened to be out in the front yard when Cousin Harold's bird dog ran up to her and started barking. She promptly lay down, rolled over on her back and sprayed an eighteen-square-foot area on the side of the house with twelve pounds of fertilizer. A remarkable feat for a seven-pound cat.

Things didn't get better, they got worse. Cleo went into heat. Now cats are not known for their modesty. But most cats go into heat, get pregnant, and that is the end of it for a few months. But not Cleo! She went into heat twice in the same month. The first round lasted about seven days. The second was the more typical two or three days. But at that point, we were beginning to wonder if Cleo ever did anything normally.

The transformation in Cleo was as awesome as the birthing process that preceded it, although not as quick. After she had kittens, she finally had a purpose in life besides eating and sleeping. Also, she seemed to have an inborn knowledge of how to take care of her offspring, which was remarkable for such a klutz. But we didn't know what a fierce mama she had turned into until our cousin came out with his dog again. The kittens were a couple of months old. The dog caught sight of his old victim and thought he would run up and bark like he had before. He never even got out a "WOOF." Instead, he let out a series of "ki-yis" as Cleo chased him under the fir tree and proceeded to thoroughly lacerate him, nose, belly and ears. The turning of the worm had begun.

Some march to a different beat but Cleo didn't even have a drummer until she had those kittens. With each succeeding litter the beat got stronger and so did the size of the litters. When the last batch was eight, the folks took her to the vet in Colfax to be spayed. This was when I found out cats can cry.

We left Cleo at the vet's for three days and when we went to pick her up she was in a terrible state. The vet said he had never seen anything like it. All the time she was there she had refused to eat and just lay in her cage meowing and crying real tears until all the hair under her eyes was gone. The vet said this didn't stop until we came through the door to pick her up.

Cleo slept all the way home. After she got home, she started eat-

95

ing. The next few days, she ate so much (and gained so much weight) we couldn't get to the stitches we were supposed to remove. We had to put her in the car to take her to the vet. Cleo started caterwauling the moment we cranked up the car and continued the whole thirty miles to Colfax. As soon as the stitches were removed and we got her back in the car, she lay down in the back seat and went to sleep for the ride back to the ranch. One strange cat.

Six months later, our family of about 20 cats was hit with feline distemper, a highly infectious and deadly disease. We lost most of the cats. I can remember wrapping one cat after another in towels and force-feeding them liver and eye droppers of aspirin. Every three or four hours around the clock we were treating a half dozen cats. Cleo seemed like she was the worst of the lot. She had the most weight loss, and she refused to eat even after others were on the road to recovery. Then one day she just started eating and doing everything normally as though nothing had happened. She acted so well she made the others look like a bunch of malingerers. But to her dying day she did not like the sight of an eye dropper.

It was after this that Cleo finally started exerting her queenly authority. She did not bully or threaten so much as refuse to yield. If she was hungry, she pushed the others aside and made them wait until she was done eating. If she wanted to sleep in the red rocker, she would jump up on the seat, lie down and then wiggle and squirm until the other cats just left or were displaced by her squirming. She had her favorite spot, right in the middle. No clawing or hissing necessary, they just knew.

As the years wore on, Cleo's crown got bigger and bigger, to the point where even we would yield to her wishes upon occasion. However, she never could get the folks to let her stay in at night. And she knew it. As soon as she saw us getting ready to retire, or heard someone say the magical words, "Well, time for bed," she would slither off whatever place she happened to be sleeping and try to hide. Then Father would act as if he couldn't find her. This used to last five or ten minutes even though her big butt would be sticking out from behind the curtains or wherever she had gone. She couldn't seem to get it through her noggin that just because her head was out of sight it didn't mean the rest of her was invisible. This evening ritual came to be as much a tradition as her always getting her very own bacon in the morning on her special plate.

Cleo graced our household for over eighteen years. She was not the brightest, nor biggest, nor prettiest, but she definitely had personality. Looking back, it was a privilege to be her subject and servant during her long and eventful reign.

T. C., A Cat's Story

Christine B. Swanson

If it were truly possible for a cat to claim a profession in our human world then T.C. would have been a Nurse and a darn good one. He seemed stern, but then that was just T.C. taking his cat career seriously. He had a no nonsense, let's get to work, get up and get over it, attitude about him. It would slightly annoy him if one only had a cold or the flu, and when he poised himself at the foot of your bed, slowly flicking his tail it meant self-pity was a waste of his time. So if I wasn't sure what was ailing me I took my diagnosis from this cat by his look and his tail action.

My husband had picked out this baby ball of fur from a litter that had been born in the basement of a farmhouse in Mission, British Columbia. He was a runt. His name came from his genetic makeup, a Tom Cat or a Tabby Cat. We could never really decide what the initials actually stood for but he was given the handle of "T. C.," and that was what we called him for all the years that he shared quarters with us.

T. C. had no choice when we first took him home. He voiced his disagreement from the moment he left the security of his mother's warm blanketed bed and the company of his comforting siblings. He had the weakest sounding "mew" and yet then, it was his strongest "plea".

He fit snugly in the palm of my husband's hand and when the fingers were gently rolled inward to form a fist all that was left of T. C. were two little ears sticking out between fingers.

He only weighed several ounces at the time of his arrival to our home. He had the notable stripes of a tabby and a gray coat with four white socks. He sported a white patch around his mouth area and had gray whiskers mixed with a few white ones that never straightened out. He was definitely cute but had missed out on the blessings of being handsome. However, to us, he had his Kodak moments.

At first his eyes only knew two formations, big and focused or completely closed, while napping. Then one evening something happened. While he was resting on an easy chair appearing as if he were only a tiny fur bump on an ocean sized cushion; he winked at us. Then we knew that he had accepted, approved, and had adopted us forever, or at least into the far side of eighteen years which was to be "forever", for him.

He did everything kittens normally do, he caught and tried to share mice prizes, he slept in the most incredulous places and ate from his dish while standing in the middle of it. What was unusual about him was his addiction to peppermint. He would cross the room in a flash with a couple of paws missing the floor if he thought he heard the crinkling of cellophane and there might be a mint some where. One Christmas morning, T. C. had the bow off, wrapping paper torn, box opened and was enjoying Russian mint chocolates, a present that should have been a surprise gift for us. So that was T. C., a typical cat but a peppermint thief.

Now somewhere between his Kittenhood and his Cathood he somehow acquired Medical Knowledge. Maybe it was our new pup, a tan and black Shepherd that was afraid of loud noises And tried to run under the house of his birthplace, away from his mother. My husband reached under the crawl space of the house and picked him up and claimed this one to come home with us. He was a runt. T. C. performed nursing type duties, caring, cleaning and watching out for him. Thank goodness T.C. had someone that finally appreciated and enjoyed every morsel of furry rodent that he caught and shared. Then T. C. took the pup hunting to learn how to get his own treasures.

Maybe his skills had been natural and Mother Nature just installed in him "compassion" and "duty" so that he had a purpose in life. Some people can go through their whole lives trying to figure out who they are but not so for cats, at least it didn't seem that way for T. C.

Now it wasn't important as to how I had acquired a serious injury but I was hospitalized in Vancouver and had surgery on my back and then was placed in a partial body cast and sent home. You can either stand up or lay down with this cast so I was taken home in an ambulance lying on a stretcher. From the time of my arrival to my house and even as the ambulance was making it's way into the carport with the back up alarm sounding T. C. took right over. He who disliked mechanical monsters let alone an alarmed one, jumped into back of this vehicle as soon as the door was opened and landed right on top of me on the stretcher. He had that "look," an expression of my mother's from years past. I almost heard "What did you do now?" and "Just where have you been?" Then he preceeded us through the open door of the house and stopped waiting, as if giving the attendants directions on which way to go by following him. I had to stay in the downstairs guest bedroom, as it was too awkward to climb the stairs. Physically I retreated to that room and T. C. moved in with me.

This was a no nonsense ordeal and since I had his full attention I knew that I had problems. I was recuperating though it was to be a long process. My husband was gone fourteen hours a day for work purposes and that left me alone. But then I wasn't really alone.

The first thing I learned as T. C.'s patient was never to close a door between him and myself. He would throw himself at the door and howl, cry, and scratch until I gave in and opened it. Sometimes he would sit in the bedroom doorway so that I couldn't shut it. Then when I was comfortably in bed he would come and go as he pleased. His night rounds, I guess. I learned to leave the bathroom door open too but not without a cat fight first. For purposes of privacy and because there was also a cool draft coming from the kitchen that made this room uncomfortable I shut the door. That too was a mistake. So I had to leave that door open as well and took up shivering. Once I even had a notion to go upstairs to the comfort of my own bed but he blocked the bottom of the stairs and I was physically unable to step around him. I think I even asked him if he could actually read minds.

He had good bedside manners. He slept with me and kept me company and not at the foot of the bed on the soft quilt but right on top of my cast. He purred and not only was the sound relaxing but it caused a gentle vibration sensation with the cast that was very soothing. How did he know that?

Well, I finally got over it and we all progressed into the next few years. We pulled up stakes and moved way up North. We brought along one protesting cat, one full sized Shepherd, a Collie and a talking Cockatiel and all went in one vehicle and we all actually survived and arrived. There was also a horse that had moved into our lives a while back and he was northward bound as well but he had his own form of transportation. After hearing T. C.'s vocal opinion about this house he forgave us and settled in for eleven years of healing in this place.

The Shepherd, the same one that T .C. taught to hunt appreciated that delicious sport. One day on the new place he hunted down what must have seemed to him to be the biggest field mouse he had ever seen. He should have however, paid more attention to his teacher because this gigantic prey attacked him and sent him home. His face was so infested with porcupine quills he couldn't even close his mouth. My husband did the needlework on him with a pair of pliers and then T. C. took over with his sandpaper tongue and nursed the wounds on his face. He cleaned and soothed and kept a watch over him. The Shepherd got sympathy and lots of cat care.

Somehow we acquired more animals. T. C. didn't care too much for the larger hoofed animals and preferred the house to the barn but when he thought he was needed he made barn calls.

We had a four month old foal that had been running and had fallen and hit her head on a gate and had given herself some type of concussion. The Veterinarian thought so as well. My husband and I stayed with her trying to keep her still and calm even though she had been sedated. T. C. came down to the barn area and checked the foal over. He stood over the sleeping foal as if examining her then after a few minutes he walked away and didn't even look back at her. He didn't glance at us either. We thought that this was kind of unusual but then we were so focused on the filly that we let the incident pass. Not for long though, as we later found out that the foal had a head injury and hairline fractures in her neck and wasn't going to survive. It had taken the Veterinarian two days of examinations and treatment and x-rays to find out what T. C. seemingly figured out in his own way in about two minutes. Then it dawned on us as to why T. C. had just walked away. There was nothing that he could do. There was nothing than anyone could do. So we lost our baby horse but found more respect for our cat.

We really didn't have any idea what it would be like to actually face the deaths with our long beloved pets.

The Shepherd was first; he died of old age in his sleep at the age of fourteen years. He wasn't sick. He just seemed to slow down, sleeping most of the time and quietly passed away.

T. C. slowed down too, a couple of years later, and that terrified us. He didn't seem to have things easy and he himself was a very bad patient. He didn't want to be nursed. He lost weight, and soon became only a shadow of his former self. He accepted a chair with a heating pad, some warm milk, soft cat food and nothing else. He took no emotional pity. Silence loomed in our home this fall for we both feared that discussions would lead to decisions. Procrastination was working for us but not for T. C. Then it became inevitable. The final day arrived bringing the final hour and minutes of T. C's life. It was a very hard decision for us to have had to make. My husband made the trip to the Veterinary clinic. T. C. was diagnosed as a very old and tired cat and mercifully put to sleep.

On the way to the animal hospital, T. C. climbed slowly up under the dashboard of the truck. Just like the ride that brought him into our lives, in a similar fashion it took him away from our lives. There was no protest this time. He was then brought home and buried on the farm where he had played, hunted and had carried out over half his life's work.

I am sure that every cat has a remarkable attribute or precious gift about him or her. I believe that everyone should live with or at least get to know one of these quizzical creatures. Sadly to say though, I don't think that there will ever be another T. C. I am sure that the likes of him will never come this way again, but just in case, hide the peppermints.

TOBY THE TIGER

Cynthia Sweeney

By nature, I have always been a squeamish person. I don't like needles, or blood, or seeing things suffer. I feel bad for the worm that goes on the end of a hook and for taking my screaming cat to the vet, even if it's for her own good.

Because I'm such a softie, every cat I've ever had has been spoiled silly. Growing up, we always had a cat, usually a Tom cat. As I had no younger siblings, the cats were my confidants and my friends. If they did not object, I dressed them up in doll clothes and pushed them around in my buggy. I liked them to sleep on my bed and curled up with them when they did. Purring motor and soft fur, together we were safe and happy.

And so, I was a very distressed five year old when Toby was missing. A striped Tom, it wasn't unusual for him to be out hunting or carousing for a couple of days. But he had been gone for ten. My mother, father and brothers had given up, but I could not stop thinking about him. It was winter in Minnesota, snow two feet deep covered the ground and temperatures dipped into the single digits, not including the wind chill. Still, every evening after supper, despite my mother's objections, she helped me into my boots and snowsuit and I searched our frozen yard for Toby, going as far as I could in the knee deep snow. I called his name and stood still in the night, the moon reflecting off the snow. It was dark and silent, nothing moved in the icy air. "Tooobbeee...." I could see my breath.

I shuddered to think what might have happened to him. Maybe he found another home and was curled up on a neighbor's hearth rug fast asleep. Or maybe he was lost, or worse yet hit by a car. Poor Toby. I hoped he was all right, and wondered if he missed me as much as I missed him.

On the tenth night the icy wind was blowing and my eyelashes had tiny bits of ice on them. I called his name and waited. Then, it happened. Over by the fence I heard something. My heart leapt and I tromped through the snow towards the noise. I could make out a shadow on the white, picket fence. He let out a strangled meow and in one lightning moment I knew that something was wrong. My heart was racing. The snow was up to my knees and I almost lost a boot but I made it back as fast as I could. "It's Toby! It's Toby!" I shouted.

In the next few confused moments, my father had brought Toby into the house. He was growling and hissing and was in a very bad mood, I can tell you that. I wanted to rush to him, to give him my love, but my mother restrained me.

"His foot's in a trap," my father said urgently. "Stay back!"

I thought of his poor little paw stuck in the fierce steel jaws. It was a raccoon trap. I heard the heavy clank of the trap as it hit the floor. Toby must have been down by the lake, which was about a half mile away, and he had dragged the painful trap behind him all the way home through the deep, frigid snow. He had tried to jump the fence but the trap got caught between the posts. I don't know how long he had been hanging there, but the thought of it still makes me cringe.

My father and brother worked a miracle, and he only lost two toes. We marveled that cats really must have nine lives, and I was very glad that Toby had eight more.

A TRAVELING CAT

Ellie S. Thomas

He was just a big, white cat and we'd come by him quite by accident. We'd recently moved and our Pride and Joy moped and moaned daily because there wasn't a child on the block for her to play with.

She looked so pathetic that we were driven to desperation, and then we heard that a co-worker had a cat he wanted to give away. It really sounded too good to be true. A full grown, male cat, well-trained, house-broken, and kind. We were skeptical.

At first glance, Freckles Freddy was impressive. He was large, probably close to fifteen pounds, and all white except for a gorgeous, plume-like tail that was inky black at the very tip as though he'd just dipped it into an ink pot. It reminded us of the plume pens artists draw on Old-Timey Christmas cards.

Freddy immediately adopted our child and began rubbing against her ankles and twining around her legs. He followed her every step, running when she ran, and crawling into her arms when she dropped down on the grass to rest. It was a case of love at first sight. We took to him right away.

But Freckles Freddy turned out to be a sly, conniving rascal. He wandered the neighborhood and spent a great deal of time outdoors and was soon infested with fleas. We reacted so strongly to the bites that I banished him outside until the vet could give me something effective; in the meantime, he learned to circumvent me in every way.

When we found him back in the house, we scolded our daughter for letting him in. Of course, she protested her innocence and was vindicated when we caught him letting himself in by the kitchen door. Who said cats aren't smart?

After that, the door was closed with special firmness. Freckles Freddy merely changed his tactics. He ran around the house and up the big old tree in the front yard. From there it was a short jump to the porch roof where one or two plaintive meows outside Mary's window did the trick and soon they were snuggled up together. When I went to rouse her for school and found him staring up at me from the pillow, I was upset...and even more angry when I saw that her body was encircled with flea bites.

Eventually, we got rid of the fleas and Freckles Freddy spent a lot more time in the house where he loved to sleep underneath the dining room table flat on his back with his feet m the air. It was a bit surprising because he looked like he'd just been embalmed but he'd always slept that way and we got used to it. A bit later on, we noticed that he balked against going outside. That was a surprise because he'd always been an outside cat, absolutely refusing to use a litter box. We couldn't figure it out because he'd go to the door and call to go out but when we opened for him, he'd pause and listen intently. If there was the slightest sound of a motor or a dog barking anywhere nearby, he'd withdraw and disappear. We figured that a dog had gotten hold of him in the recent past, or he'd been struck by a snow sled, because he developed a huge abcess beneath his jaw and the poor cat nearly died. He lay about and went off his food. I purchased delicacies and even put his food through the blender so he could eat more easily but until the large sac broke, he was a sick fellow.

To our relief, and happiness, Freckles Freddy got better and we started out on our postponed trip to a nearby city. We'd arranged for his care with a responsible neighbor and the last we saw of him he was standing on our front steps as we drove off. We would soon find out that he'd outwitted us again!

We spent the night about two hundred miles from home and it was bitterly cold. The following day we shopped awhile and then began the return trip. About half-way home, we stopped for a coffee break and when we pulled into the restaurant lot, the pitiful sounds of a cat issued from somewhere in the car. I looked at my spouse in horror. "Stop," I cried, "we've run over a cat! We're dragging it along! Stop the car!"

My husband pulled into a parking lot and stopped. The cat's yowls were now very, loud. My spouse raised the hood and looked around beneath but we could see nothing unusual. Puzzled, we decided to go inside and have a cup of coffee, hoping that if there was a cat in there someplace, it would feel safe to emerge and go away if we left it alone.

We emerged from the restaurant about a half hour later and started the last lap of our journey. The cold intensified and as Murphy's Law prevailed, we had a blow-out about forty miles from home. We were on a lonely stretch and had no options but to change the tire ourselves. As my spouse worked on the tire, the cat tuned up again and became very vocal. It was a night to remember with the shuddering cold, the cat yowling like a banshee, and our teeth clattering like castanets.

Eventually we got back to town and when we sped down our street and into the driveway, our daughter looked out the window for her cat. Then it struck her.

"That's Freckles Freddy in the car. That's my cat. Get him out, Daddy, get him out!"

We stared at her as though she'd lost her mind. What was wrong with the child? It couldn't possibly be her cat, could it?

It was.

Once the serviceman had removed parts of the grill and horn, we dragged Freckles Freddy out of the curl of the fender, apparently none the worse for wear. We kept him in the house for a few days after his travel until we thought he could be trusted outside again. We watched him explore the yard. He seemed content but the next day, he was gone again.

We advertised for him and alerted the telephone men, the postman, and the garbage collectors, but he'd vanished. He'd apparently had his fill of the chilly North.

We can only assume that Freckles Freddy has hitched another ride and is probably soaking up sunshine somewhere in the Florida Keys. So, now that you know what he looks like, and what his habits are, if you should find him, we'd appreciate it if you'd kindly help him get on the right bus for home.

END OF AN ERA

Ellen Vayo

After I check in, I choose the only secluded seat in the waiting room, the chair between the giant stuffed Saint Bernard and the equally large aquarium, the chair farthest from the commotion of fidgety children, frustrated mothers and quivering dogs on short leashes.

Across from me, a young woman with a pinched-in waist strokes a kitten. I want to tell her to appreciate the wild-eyed tiny puff of fur batting at her gaudy Christmas earrings. That kitten will never again be the same as it is right this moment, never as playful, fur never as shiny, reflexes never as fast. Beginnings are such fun. I wish my Molly were a kitten again with life brightly stretching out in front of her.

Funny how I didn't notice the years passing so quickly. Didn't notice Father Time robbing me of the tiny half-drowned kitten I'd pulled from the river and fed with an eyedropper.

I turn from the kitten with a future and read the titles of the brochures tucked into the plastic holder attached to the wall. Molly shifts beneath the Garfield blanket on my lap, pokes her head out, gazes at me and mews, soundlessly. I rub her ears and start her purr-motor. "You've been a good friend, Mollygocatly. You're a splendidly worn cat."

I tilt Molly's head upward and kiss her mottled kitty-cat lips. She nuzzles into me, wraps her yellow paws around my hand--puts a big dent in my heart. "We've always been there for one another haven't we old girl?"

Molly was my cuddly-warmth through the loss of my breasts, a near divorce and empty nest syndrome. When Molly gave birth to her only litter, I was in the closet with her. I nursed her through spaying, hairballs and feline acne.

I catch the woman with the pinched-in waist staring at me. She forces a half smile and averts her gaze. The young never think they'll grow old, never think their kittens will mellow. I wish that weren't so wrong.

I gaze down at the cat I've shared a pillow with for more years than I've been married. The cat whose name is included at the end of all my letters and who once received a credit card with a thousand dollar limit.

"Molly." I jiggle the treasure on my lap. "Molly, remember how you loved to ride on the dashboard?" Rode there, in the sunlight, from Point Barrow Alaska to the Texas oil fields.

"Remember the winter we were so broke?" Lived on macaroni and cheese. Breakfast, lunch and dinner. Yuck! Thought we'd get the scurvy.

"And remember how I cried when we had to give up that warm-cozy farm house and move into that drafty-makeshift yurt?" The move didn't bother Miss Mollygocatly. Cats know how to adjust. She just climbed into the bottom of my sleeping bag and stayed there until she heard an envelope of cheese being ripped open.

Molly was easy. She never demanded more than a spot of sunlight and a good old belly rub. In turn, she rewarded us with stiffened squirrels at our feet, frightened, peeping birds on our pillows, and once and once only, a rat in my bubble bath.

My old Molly has slept on the kitchen table for so many years I've come to think of her as a centerpiece. She's always in the midst of everything: lying on the edge of the bathtub dipping her tail into the suds, chasing water beads as they roll down the shower door, sitting on the washer talking cat talk while I fold laundry, walking the countertop while dinner is being prepared, chasing the broom, the dust rag, the vacuum cord. She's the first to greet company when the doorbell rings. How can life be without my Molly? I stroke the mass of love on my lap, feel her ribs, her sharp spine.

"Mollygocatly, wake up," I say louder than I've intended. She opens her eyes and purrs but doesn't lift her head. "Molly, remember the fit you threw when I left on my honeymoon without you? Remember how you broke my only lamp, shredded the drapes, ate two of Roy's goldfish and terrorized old Peep-Peep into a featherless lump of lunacy?"

The receptionist steps through the half door holding a chart, glances around the room. I wince. My breath is caught somewhere between my throat and the pit of my stomach. I feel as though my heart just flipped over backwards. "Miss Roberts," she says. "We're ready for Sweety Pie. Room two." The woman with the pinched-in waist stands and walks by, smiling, with her kitten clutched to her.

Molly's damp nose touches my hand. My breath comes back in jagged gasps. Ooof, I hear myself sigh. I'm not ready for this. I can't do it. I stand and gather Molly to my chest. Her body twitches. She moans and stares up at me. I run my nose through her fur, breathe in the soft scent of perfumed litter and the stench of pain. I don't want to do this, but I can't let her go on suffering. She's been too good a friend. We settle back into the chair next to the aquarium, beneath the stare of the oversized stuffed dog.

"Now what was I saying, Molly? Oh yeah, the honeymoon, old Peep-Peep. Remember how you hid under the bed for days, pouting? Wouldn't come out even for sardines." Good old Molly, when she finally came out, she pooped in Roy's work boots, and then scooted across the paperwork he had strewn on the kitchen table.

Molly probably never knew I saved two of her nine lives that day.

"Sue, we're ready for you." The receptionist studies the papers on her clipboard. She doesn't look at us. She can't. She knows us too well. "Room three," she says. "Doctor will be right with you." I swallow and nod. I stand, but can barely make my feet move.

I take a seat in room three. My nostrils flare. The room smells of urine, disinfectant and fear. I arrange Molly on my lap, fuss with the Garfield blanket that covers her, scratch her throat. Through the wall, I hear a woman laugh. I lean sideways to pick up on the muffled one sided conversation being held in baby talk. "You'll never grow old will you my silly Sweety Pie?"

I kiss Molly between the ears and nod my head toward the wall. "Youth in denial," I say. That woman's joy comes naturally. She's grateful her kitten just needs shots, maybe wormed, but all the same healthy.

Doctor Peters comes in, closes the door behind her and leans back against it. She stuffs her hands into the pockets of her medical jacket. A white ring circles her mouth. She doesn't like this part of her job. The bantering and niceties we usually exchange are shelved, instead, she asks if I'd like to wait in my car. "I'll bring her to you when I'm finished."

I say nothing. I try, but I can't speak. I shake my head. She turns away, fills a hypodermic syringe with solution, taps it, pushes the plunger. Fluids spray into the air.

I squeeze my prize. "Good-bye Mollygocatly," I say, soundlessly. She mews and gazes up at me. Her eyes are soft and yielding, clouded with cataracts and trust.

CAT SENSE

Christine Watt

"That cat's acting strangely, isn't he, Tinty?" asked Da, peering over the tops of his reading glasses. He held the newspaper open, distracted from headlines of death and destruction by the decidedly odd goings-on of Monsieur Bilbo Baggins, who simply would not let me leave the house.

I was due at rehearsal in New York City in an hour. I had to leave now. But Monsieur Bilbo Baggins would have none of it as he guarded the door screaming the way only a Siamese can. I tried to open the door, but he planted himself so I'd squash his toes if I persevered. I picked him up to hand to Mam, but he wrapped my head in his front legs and dug his claws into my shoulders. I couldn't peel him off. This was worse than when I took him to the vet. I didn't understand it at all; he'd never behaved like this before. Normally when I left for rehearsal, he adopted the "See if I care" attitude cats convey so well. Then when I returned, I got a nonchalant "So what?" for some considerable time, which I thought pretty rich coming from a rescue cat.

At last I prized his paws away and handed him to Mam, whom normally he adored, but he leaped with a shriek from her as if he'd landed on a hot-plate. He twined around my ankles until I smacked down on my bottom with a thump.

"He doesn't want you to leave, does he?" said Da, puzzled.

Mam frowned and commented, "Peculiar."

"If he doesn't get better after I've gone," I called over a protesting Monsieur Bilbo Baggins as I carried him to the kitchen and fastened him in, "would you call the vet, please? I'll be back as soon as I can. Let him have the run of the house as soon as I've gone, won't you?"

Mam nodded and said, "Have a nice time, pet."

"Ta-ta," said Da, returning to the paper.

It was great having Mam and Da here. They were visiting from their sleepy village in England while my husband was on a lengthy business trip to the Far East.

I escaped to the garage and drove down our driveway. Monsieur Bilbo Baggins leaped from window to window following me, yowling so loudly I could hear him through the storm windows. I was baffled. He was acting the same way he had over Bugsy dog's leg. He'd screamed at that leg for days until one day Bugsy stood up and yelped in agony as out shot the leg uncontrollably. A visit to the vet revealed a tumor. Fortunately we caught it in time. I shook my head and headed for the Lincoln Tunnel that would take me from New Jersey to Manhattan under the Hudson River.

Rehearsal was in the Ansonia Hotel, that Mecca for music-lovers where Caruso had once stayed, and amazingly I found a parking spot on nearby Riverside Drive. I wasn't sure if I was parked legally so got out of the car to check parking signs. After studying them, I was none the wiser but decided to risk it until I could ask somebody at rehearsal. I almost asked three young men passing by, but they were walking too quickly. I set off along the sidewalk in the opposite direction, going over my part in my head. I'd just rounded the corner into 73rd Street when the nightmare began.

"Give me money." One of the young men blocked my way, his two friends either side of me, very close.

I thought they must have to make a phone call. "You need a dime?" I asked with a smile, reaching into my bag.

A gun was thrust under my nose. I wondered why. Was this some kind of joke? Why would three total strangers want to shoot me? I'd never done them any harm, I'd never done anybody any harm that I could think of, I was even a vegan so I wouldn't harm any living being. It must be one of those Candid Camera scenarios. A little flag would pop out of the gun proclaiming, "Bang," and we'd all have a jolly good laugh.

They must have thought I was resisting handing over my money or I was going for a gun in my bag because the next thing I knew the biggest one grasped my coat lapels in one fist. I was helpless as a rag doll as he lifted me up off the ground. The one with the gun looked nervous, wild-eyed, the gun shaking as he jabbed it in my face. A vision of Mam sobbing over a hospital cot where I lay with half a head flashed before my mind's eye and I prayed silently, "Let them kill me not make me a vegetable."

The man who'd picked me up pulled his other fist way back. He was going to hit me. As his knuckles swooped down out of the sky at me, I swung my head away and took the brunt of the blow in my cheek socket rather than on the jaw, but it knocked my glasses off and needles of light orbited my skull. I'd never been hit by a man. I knew men packed a lot of strength in their shoulders, but I had no idea they could inflict this much pain with one bare-knuckle punch. I slumped over the fire hydrant, felt my bag being tugged from my arm . . . and finally woke up.

His skin touching mine was what did it. How dare he! I'd been raised with a strong sense of indignation at injustice and sensed some unstoppable power uncoiling inside me, hot, roiling, murderous, lashing and snapping, surging upward blinding me to danger. I don't think I've ever known such anger before or since. I could have bitten their heads off.

With hindsight this was the most stupid reaction for a lone young woman against three strapping men, but being set upon in this way had aroused something primeval in me.

I didn't mention what sort of rehearsal I was going to. Opera. I'd vocalized for a good hour before leaving the house so my voice was warmed up. I couldn't fight these men their way, but fight them I would.

I wheeled around, opened my throat like a funnel, and roared into their faces. They leaped sky-high. I hope I shattered their ear drums. As they fled from my outrage--I was a contralto but hit several high C's that day--I chased them, attacking with my voice, which seemed to drag me along after it as I tore around the corner pursuing them up Riverside Drive, beating them to a pulp with Wagnerian decibels. As they outran me, I roared out my frustration at not being able to lay my bare hands on them, across the Hudson, down to the New York City Opera, up to heaven.

A window way up a towering skyscraper flung open. "Enough already, lady," boomed a voice. "I called the cops. I told them some broad's being murdered in the street. Pipe down, will ya?"

I hadn't realized I was still bellowing. It's a wonder that both lungs hadn't come flying out of my mouth. I slumped against the wall, totally drained.   I was reduced to one great shuddering pulse, pounding as if I had fever.

A hand clawed at my elbow. "Come!   I'm a doctor."

My head jerked around to look at a seedy specimen clutching my coat arm telling me he was a doctor. A likely story. My sixth sense told me this situation was more dangerous than what I'd just survived. And suddenly I remembered Monsieur Bilbo Baggins's reaction to my coming here tonight. His cat sense had foreseen all.

"We saw everything," rasped another man's voice, out of breath, panting. "We were driving up Riverside Drive. Are you all right, dear?"

I wheeled around on this second man and instantly felt safer. He was older, bundled up for winter, taking my arm in a different way from the "doctor." I buzzed around again, and my doctor had disappeared.

"My son's going after them," said the kind man.

I looked up Riverside Drive to see a young man tearing along the sidewalk. I pulled away from his father and rushed after him. "No," I yelled. "They've got a gun. Come back, please, it's not worth it."

The son stopped and trotted back to me. He and his father helped me into the nearest building, where I collapsed on a seat in the vestibule. Somebody handed me a Styrofoam cup of water. I don't know why people administer water at times like this. It was winter, the water was cold. But I suppose they want to do something, anything to show concern.

"Where was the Neighborhood Watch!" barked one tenant.

"That's the third time this week somebody's been mugged on this corner," complained another.

"It's a disgrace."

"Something ought to be done about it."

Quite a crowd had gathered. Contrary to the experience of many New Yorkers, my cries had not gone unheeded. I was the center of a lot of folks' attention that evening, while the police drove up in a matter of minutes.

Before I crawled into the police car to scout around the streets to see if we could spot my muggers, a frail old lady tottered up to me and stared into my face as if scrutinizing it for signs of injury.

She demanded in a quavering voice, "Where did you learn to scream like that?"

"I'm sorry, something sort of took over, I---"

"You're sorry! Are you kidding, hon'? Boy, I wish I could scream like that. Maybe then those bastards would have left me alone when they jumped me last week with a knife at my throat." She dragged an arthritic forefinger across her wrinkled neck with a gallows grimace.

I looked into her rheumy eyes and began to cry. As if sensing that my life was no longer threatened, whatever animal instinct had taken hold of me to ensure I lived retreated to its lair, and I started shivering as if somebody had dipped me in ice-water. I could have been killed. To reinforce that terrible truth, my jaw sprang alive with pain, my tongue poked among loosened teeth, and I swallowed the ferrous taste of my own blood. I could be dead. I wanted nothing more in life at that moment than to be at home with Mam and Da, the dogs, and the glorious, the magnificent Monsieur Bilbo Baggins.

Of course the police and I didn't sight the muggers. The police offered to drive me to a hospital but I refused, I had to get home. They dropped me at the Ansonia. Another cast member drove me home, joking that Beverly Sills was probably searching the streets right now for the new diva of the high C's. Da flew downstairs hitting one step in six, declaring he was going to buy a gun and shoot every bloke in New York City that very night.

"Have a cup of tea first, dear," muttered Mam as she wandered upstairs in a daze. The British answer to every eventuality is a hot cup of tea--funerals, births, marriages, war, muggings. If ever the world is faced with annihilation, while other nations indulge in missile launches, self-flagellation, orgies, we Brits shall be boiling water for one last cuppa. It's a comforting thought somehow.

I wondered why Mam was going upstairs to make the tea, but I didn't say anything. I couldn't anyway because my jaws wouldn't open. Eventually she staggered downstairs, still in shock, and found the kitchen.

I tumbled onto the couch, a steaming mug of tea--with drinking straw--made by Mam on the coffee table in front of me. Da, having been persuaded not to go and get himself slain, cradled me in his arms. The dogs lay protectively at my feet. And Monsieur Bilbo Baggins, far from cold-shouldering me, crawled up my battered body kneading my flesh, pummeling with velvet pads, pounding me with affection, purring like an engine as he rubbed his head so hard against the side of my face that wasn't damaged it's a wonder I didn't wake up next morning with bruising on both cheeks.

Now I have the sense never to ignore cat sense.

SUNSHINE

Garnet Hunt White

His gleaming, golden fur as sunny as sunlight gave Sunshine his name. It also sets him apart from other cats. His hair has a silky soft feel like lush-plush velvet.

His fleecy milk white feet are fluffy like down. He looks at the other cats; cocks his head sideways; then follows me. That is, he follows me until he becomes the boss.

Sunshine purrs then peers at me through golden green eyes. He leads me towards his cat pan, stops before he gets there, turns his head and scrutinizes me. I follow.

He turns up his nose at yesterday's food. I put fresh dry food in his pan. He eyes me, then turns as I open him a can of chicken and liver to fill his dish. He eats. I fill his water bowl and add a couple of ice cubes. He has me well trained.

Sunshine takes me to whichever door he chooses to pass through when he wants to go outside. He scratches on the French Doors when he decides to come in. I spring from my chair and open the door. He walks in, head held high, tail straight up. He has me under his paw.

When Glenn, my husband, would come home from work, Sunshine would then transfer his affections to him. He never failed to accompany him into the walk-in closet. He smelled, then walked to Glenn's house shoes, and pulled them forward with his paw.

When Glenn would settle down in his chair to read, Sunshine would curl up on the back of his chair, put his head on Glenn's shoulder and nap. During the day, when I worked at my computer, he always quietly curled in my lap.

Many times I have heard Glenn laugh as he looked out the south window. I asked, "Why are you laughing?"

Glenn would say, "There goes Sunshine up the hill to check the menu at Doctor Gene and Mary's house." Or he would say, "Sunshine's coming down the hill. He's checked out Doctor's place." These travels of Sunshine brought about a nickname, The Partnership Cat.

When Sunshine feels left out, he reaches a white paw out and grabs my skirt. I take him in my arms and stroke his velvety fur. That satisfies him.

Sunshine has hobbies. He likes to ride in the car, sleep on the car's roof in the garage, and watch television, especially the cat food commercials where the cats swish across the screen.

One day, Sunshine and I strolled across our back yard, which joins the Mark Twain National Forest. I carried my bucket for picking greens.

Sunshine stopped and made a blood curdling noise deep in his throat. I stopped and looked at him. Oh! The velvet fur stood straight outward from his body. His back arched high like a rainbow. His eyes slanted. What was he looking at?

I stood still and looked toward the woods. A second later, I saw two coyotes just outside the fence. I yelled and threw my salad bucket at the fence. They disappeared.

"Oh, Sunshine." I hugged him. "You sure paid for your keeps

today."

He purred then laid his head on my shoulders.

Glenn suddenly passed away with a heart attack. A stunned shock gripped me. I couldn't sleep; I couldn't eat. Exhausted, but I had to carry on. I lay on the bed at night hoping to rest.

I would become aware of a breathing, purring by my pillow. Sunshine would be laying on the bed near my head. He had never slept on our bed before. He stroked my hair with his paw. Glenn always stroked my hair before he went to sleep. How did Sunshine know to do this?

I took Sunshine to the cemetery. He jumped out of the car, went to Glenn's grave, turned around three time, and laid down.

Yes, Sunshine demands his satisfying food, to be petted, and to be king of the house.

But Sunshine has changed since Glenn's passing. He doesn't take all. He knows how to give by walking away from his cat food in favor of another cat. He shows how to comfort by letting a kitten snuggle up to him to sleep. He is patience with me when I'm slow to feed him.

I don't understand how Sunshine knows so much about me, a human life, but he has helped make my lonely days more bearable.

Through Sunshine, I've learned to have more respect, respect for him, respect for all cats, both the discarded ones, and the loved ones.

There's a bond between Sunshine and me. Love. We love each other. We give our love to others.

THE KEYS

Lucy L. Woodward

There is a wing-backed pale green chair by the sideboard in our living room that catches the afternoon sunlight. I'm tired and I lie on the couch. Our gray cat drapes over the arm like a carelessly dropped fur stole, rubbing her chin around its curving end until she peers at me upside down, ears pointing toward the rug and sunlight soaking her white underbelly.

Our dog finds her curious, stimulating, full of the devil. A small, blonde American Husky, he jumps onto the chair and sits on her. They look at each other. The cat slithers out from under him and climbs up the winged back to walk its edge with pristine grace.

The dog watches her fixedly.

That's impossible, I hear him think. No one can walk such a narrow edge. He looks at me. Can they?

I smile, but I don't say anything. It's obvious someone can.

She tenses, poised; he observes her from the chair seat. What will she do? He knows and so do I. What else but leap? As primitive as an atavism. As certain as gravity. If a cat crouches, ready, nothing short of distraction can stop her.

Or a sudden thought. Lots of times I've been ready to have fun, then stopped by a cautious thought. But she doesn't think, they say.

I say she does.

She eyes the sideboard. She knows shiny keys are in the slightly opened drawer. She leaps, and the dog's ears flick in satisfaction. He pulls forward with his front paws, hoisting himself farther over the chair arm to watch her. The cat reaches a paw into the drawer, and with the barest flick of feline fingernails, pulls out my Chevy keys and lets them drop to a sunspot on the rug. She drops to light over them, pinning them with yellow black vertical slitted eye.

She picks them up, tosses them, worries them like a mouse, and neither sees nor thinks of anything else.

But the dog does. He knows they're keys. He looks at me. He jumps down and walks to me like a worried older brother.

She's got the keys. She might lose them. Make her put them back again.

She can't put them back, I think. She's only a cat.

I would have to put them back myself because I'm a grown-up human person. I have to get some work done. Stop dreaming about a sunspot on the living room floor and two beautiful creatures bathed in innocence. I have to be responsible. But maybe once in a while it would be all right if I just played in a spot of sun on the floor. God wouldn't mind.

LAZY CAT THAT SAVED $200,000

Lucille White

Winner of the Preservation Foundation Cat Story Contest
which ran from January 1, 1997, to December 31, 2000

The lazy cat was a plump black and white animal named Perezosa, which means "lazy" in Spanish, so she was aptly named. She was a South American and seafaring feline. The motion of the ship never bothered her, but she seldom moved unless it was to get more comfortable. It was by her laziness she saved the Estrella Navigation Company of Valparaiso 625,000 pesos which at that time amounted to $200,000 in our currency.

The name of the ship was Perla del Sud, captained by Agosto Fuentes. Perezosa was not only the mascot of the ship but the pride and joy of the captain even if she was not a good mouser and the crew complained about her laziness. They wanted a new mascot, especially one who would keep the rats and mice from taking over the ship.

At times other cats were brought on board but when the captain found out about them, they were quickly put ashore at the first opportunity for no cat, under any conditions, was going to take the place of his lazy, but beloved, Perezosa.

One night bound for Callao, Peru, out of Valparaiso, carrying a heavy load of mining machinery, a storm came down upon the ship. It was so violent that the cargo broke loose. It was later learned, at a hearing, that the freight had arrived late and the workers had done a rushed job in getting it aboard. Once it broke loose, the crew did the best they could to secure it but were not having much luck, so they decided to rig what is called a sea anchor and just ride it out. But even that did not work. The storm was too violent, pitching them all over the place.

It broke the captain's heart, but he had no choice when the ship began to leak and settle deeper down into the water. He gave the orders to abandon ship. In all the excitement, it was only after all the lifeboats had pulled away that Captain Fuentes realized his beloved Perezosa had been left on the ship!

On getting to shore and safety, the injured were sent to hospitals and the rest of the crew was sent back to Valparaiso. Captain Fuentes grieved about Perezosa until he heard the news that a tug had salvaged his ship. She had not sunk after all!

But there was bad news, the company that owned the tug boat was now demanding salvage money from the Estrella Navigation Company. An amount of 650,000 pesos! An amount that would not only wreck his company but that would deprive Captain Fuentes of a ship!

But if the ship had not sunk, then Perezosa could still be alive! Captain Fuentes immediately went to Taltal, where the ship had been towed, to find out if Perezosa was indeed still alive. He found her in the care of the tugboat man, who handed her over, saying he had never seen the likes of her. She had evidently never left the cabin of the Perla del Sud until the ship had been tied up at the docks.

Upon hearing that, Captain Fuentes got excited and asked the tugman if he was absolutely sure about that. The tugman swore it was so, and wondered why the captain was so elated over being told that about Perezosa.

Captain Fuentes immediately wired the owners of the Estrella Navigation Company that he had good news. And it was good news, for it meant that the settlement to the tugboat company would only be for the towing charges, which amounted to only 25,000 pesos. Their claim of 650,000 pesos was thrown out because the ship, Perla del Sud, had not been found a derelict "without a living creature."

Perezosa had been very much alive, even if she had probably been asleep the whole time. Captain Fuentes gave his beloved Perezosa a gentle hug. By being too lazy to get off a ship everyone believed to be sinking, she had protected the Estrella Company's property rights and proved to one and all that she was, indeed, a good luck mascot.

May 7, 2001
Nashville, Tennessee

Ordering Information

Books are $10 each (US currency) plus shipping costs. There are price discounts at five and twenty five copies. Discounts are available to bookstores, libraries, churches, and other nonprofit organizations.

Contact us for detailed information.

Order books by telephone:
Call Richard Loller at 1 800 228-8517 or 615 269-2433.

Order by fax:
Attn: Richard Loller
615-269-2440.

Order by E-mail:
preserve@storyhouse.org

You can also order from our web site using your credit card. Go to:
http://www.storyhouse.org/orders.html

We invite you to visit our web site and read all the 153 entries in the contest: http://www.storyhouse.org